Getting Past No

Getting
past
no

Negotiating with difficult people

William Ury

RANDOM HOUSE
BUSINESS BOOKS

Copyright © William Ury 1991

The right of William Ury to be identified as the author of this work has
been asserted by him in accordance with the Copyright, Designs and
Patents Act 1988

First published in Great Britain in 1991 by
Business Books Limited
This edition published in 1992 by Century Business
An imprint of Random Century Limited
20 Vauxhall Bridge Road, Londoon SW1V 2SA

Twenty Eigth Impression 2012

Random Century Australia (Pty) Limited
20 Alfred Street, Milsons Point, Sydney
New South Wales 2061, Australia

Random Century New Zealand Limited
18 Poland Road, Glenfield
Auckland 10, New Zealand

Random House (Pty) Limited
Isle of Houghton, Corner of Boundary Road & Carse O'Gowrie,
Houghton 2198, South Africa

Random House Publishers India Private Limited
301 World Trade Tower, Hotel Intercontinental Grand Complex,
Barakhamba Lane, New Delhi 110 001, India

Research at Harvard University is undertaken with the expectation of
publication. In such publication, the authors alone are responsible for
statements of fact, opinions, recommendations and conclusions expressed.
Publication in no way implies approval or endorsement by Harvard
University, any of its faculties, or by the President and Fellows of Harvard
College.

Printed and bound by CPI Group (UK) Ltd, Croydon, CR0 4YY

Britsh Library Cataloguing in Publication Data
A catalogue record for this book is available from the British Library

ISBN 9780712655231

For Roger Fisher
with gratitude

Contents

Getting Past No

Author's Note

Ten years ago Roger Fisher and I wrote a book called *Getting to Yes,* which presented a step-by-step "dance routine" for negotiating mutually satisfactory agreements. That book continues to have considerable appeal, but there are questions almost every reader ends up asking: "What if the other side hasn't read your book? What if they won't dance that way? What if their answer is *no?*"

Getting Past No responds to these tough questions. I have tried to distill the techniques of successful negotiation in difficult situations into an all-purpose, five-step method called "breakthrough negotiation." If *Getting to Yes* outlines a dance routine, *Getting Past No* shows how to get a reluctant partner to dance. While the two books complement each other, each stands on its own. You don't need to have read the earlier book in order to understand and appreciate this one.

In writing this book I faced several troublesome language problems. What should the difficult person be called? "The other person" seemed too bland, while "adversary" risked reinforcing a win-lose mindset. In the end, I have relied principally on the term "your opponent." By definition, "opponent" doesn't mean an enemy but simply someone who has taken a position opposite to yours.

Then there was the question of pronouns. Should the opponent be "he" or "she"? I tried interchanging "she" and "he," but readers found it confusing. At last I fell back on using "he" and "him" as generic pronouns. I apologize to any readers offended by this usage.

In working on successive drafts, I often felt like the opera tenor whose finale was greeted with enthusiastic cries of "Encore! Encore!" After the fifth encore, the tenor asked the audience, "How many more times do you want me to sing?" And the answer came back: "Until you get it right!"

My audience has been equally demanding. I am immensely grateful for the comments and suggestions of those who read drafts, including Linda Antone, James Botkin, William Breslin, Nancy Buck, Stephen Goldberg, Richard Haass, Deborah Kolb, Linda Lane, David Lax, Martin Linsky, David Mitchell, Bruce Patton, John Pfeiffer, John Richardson, Carol Rinzler, Jeffrey Rubin, James Sebenius, Dayle Spencer, William Spencer, Daniel Stern, Douglas Stone, Elizabeth Ury, and Janice Ury.

I should also mention my enormous debt to the Program on Negotiation at Harvard Law School. Over more than a decade my colleagues there have provided me with intellectual stimulation and camaraderie. My ideas on negotiation have been forged and tested in the freewheeling seminars and conversations that take place under the Program's hospitable roof.

Another Harvard colleague and friend, Ronald Heifetz, generously allowed me to use his evocative phrase "going to the balcony," a metaphor for taking a step back and getting some perspective.

I would also like to thank two able research assistants.

Sarah Jefferys and Annette Sassi rummaged through the Harvard libraries for relevant books and articles, assiduously collecting negotiation examples. In addition, Annette wrote many insightful memos commenting on the evolving manuscript.

Throughout the process my assistant Sheryl Gamble proved indefatigable, working around the clock to help me meet publisher's deadlines. With unfailing good spirits she managed successive crises and kept my office under control.

Without my agent, Raphael Sagalyn, there might not have been a book. He urged me to move my work on *Getting Past No* from the back burner to the front, provided valuable feedback, and put me together with Bantam.

Bantam's fine team improved the book considerably. It has been a privilege to work with Genevieve Young, a superlative editor who took the time to coach and coax me through endless drafts. Danelle McCafferty, my line editor, applied her skillful pencil to the finished manuscript and cheered me along through the last stretch. Betsy Cenedella provided meticulous copy editing.

Let me end with a personal note. Shortly before I began writing this book, I had the great fortune to marry Elizabeth Sherwood. Little did I realize that she came from a family of determined and devoted editors. Dorothy, Richard, and Benjamin Sherwood marked up each successive draft with skill and savvy. Elizabeth read the book aloud with me from start to finish, making it leaner and more lucid. My greatest debt is to her: Her love and support got me past *Getting Past No*.

William Ury
January 1991
Santa Fe, New Mexico

Overview

Negotiating with Difficult People

Diplomacy is the art of letting someone else have *your* way.
—DANIELE VARE, Italian diplomat

Daily life is full of negotiations that can drive you crazy. Over breakfast you get into an argument with your spouse about buying a new car. You think it's time, but your spouse says, "Don't be ridiculous! You know we can't afford it right now."

You arrive at work for a morning meeting with your boss. You present him with a carefully prepared proposal for a new project, but he interrupts you after a minute and says, "We already tried that and it didn't work. Next item."

During your lunch hour you try to return a defective toaster-oven, but the salesperson refuses to refund your money because you don't have the sales slip: "It's store policy."

In the afternoon you bring an already-agreed-upon contract to a client for his signature. You have trumpeted the deal to your associates and made the necessary arrangements with manufacturing. But your client tells you: "I'm sorry. My boss refuses to okay the purchase unless you give us a fifteen percent discount."

On your drive home you flip on the radio, only to learn that yet another airplane has been hijacked by terrorists who threaten to kill all the passengers unless the government meets their demands. You feel sympathy for the families of the hostages but wonder out loud how anybody can negotiate with madmen.

In the evening you need to return some phone calls, but the line is tied up by your thirteen-year-old daughter. Exasperated, you ask her to get off the phone. She yells, "Why don't you get me my own phone line? All my friends have them." You try to reason with her, but she slams her door.

Each of us has had to face tough negotiations with an irritable spouse, an ornery boss, a rigid salesperson, a tricky customer, or an impossible teenager. Under stress, even nice, reasonable people can turn into angry, intractable opponents. Negotiations can bog down or break down, consuming our time, keeping us awake at night, and giving us ulcers.

These kinds of situations call for more than just ordinary negotiation skills. How do you deal with someone who won't listen to you? Someone who throws a temper tantrum in order to get his way? Someone who tells you: "Take it or leave it!"

How do you handle someone who constantly interrupts you? Or who accuses you of being unreliable and incompetent? Or who tries to make you feel guilty? Or who threatens you with dire consequences unless you give in?

How do you negotiate with someone who uses false, phony, or confusing information? Someone who leads you to believe you have an agreement, only to make yet another last-minute demand? Or who drags his feet endlessly? Or who just plain refuses to negotiate?

Ideally, you would engage the other person in a game of problem-solving negotiation. You would begin by identifying his interests—his concerns, needs, and desires. You would proceed to explore different options for meeting both sides' interests. Your goal would be to reach a mutually satisfactory agreement in an efficient and amicable fashion.

But what if your opponent is not interested in this kind of negotiation? You may want to get to yes, but what if his answer is no? How do you get *past* no?

Five Challenges

To get past no, you need to understand what lies behind the "no." What makes your opponent refuse to cooperate? It is easy to believe that stonewalling, attacks, and tricks are just part of his basic nature, and that there is little you can do to change his difficult behavior. But you *can* affect his behavior if you can deal successfully with his underlying motivations.

Behind your opponent's attacks may lie anger and hostility. Behind his rigid positions may lie fear and distrust. Convinced he is right and you are wrong, he may refuse to listen. Seeing the world as eat-or-be-eaten, he may feel justified in using nasty tactics to defend or avenge himself.

Further, your opponent may dig in and attack, not because he is unreasonable but because he knows no other way to negotiate. He is merely using the conventional negotiating tactics he first learned in the sandbox. In his eyes, the only alternative is to give in—and he doesn't want to do that.

Even if he is aware of the possibility of cooperative negotiation, he may spurn it because he does not see how it will benefit him. Even if you can satisfy his interests, he may be afraid of losing face as he backs down from his position. And if it is *your* idea, he may reject it for that reason alone.

Moreover, if he regards negotiation as a win-lose proposition, he will be determined to come out the winner. Feeling more powerful, he may not see why he should engage in problem-solving negotiation. He may be guided by the precept "What's mine is mine. What's yours is negotiable."

Frustrated and angered by your opponent's intransigence, you may feel like striking back. Unfortunately, this will probably provoke him even further. Or you may feel like giving in just to get him off your back. However, not only will you lose, but he may be encouraged to demand more. The problem you are up against is not only your opponent's behavior but your reaction, which can easily perpetuate the very behavior you would like to stop.

To get past no, you must overcome each of these barriers to cooperation: *his* negative emotions, *his* negotiating habits, *his* skepticism about the benefits of agreement, *his* perceived power, and *your* reaction. You thus face five challenges.

The first step is to control your own behavior. Instead of reacting, you need to regain your mental balance and stay focused on achieving what you want. The first challenge is *Don't react.*

Next you need to help your opponent regain *his* mental balance. You need to defuse his negative emotions—his defensiveness, fear, suspicion, and hostility. You need to break through his resistance and get him to listen. The second challenge is to *Disarm your opponent.*

Once you have created a favorable negotiating climate, you need to get your opponent to stop bargaining over positions and start exploring ways to meet both sides' interests. You need to break through his stone walls, deflect his attacks, and neutralize his tricks. The third challenge is to *Change the game.*

Once you have engaged your opponent in problem-solving negotiation, you need to overcome his skepticism and guide him to a mutually satisfactory agreement. You need to bridge the gap between his interests and yours. You need to help him save face and make the outcome appear as a victory for him. The fourth challenge is to *Make it easy to say yes.*

Your opponent may still believe, however, that he can prevail through superior power. You need to enhance your negotiating power and use it to bring him to the table. You need to deploy your power without making him an enemy who resists you even more. The fifth challenge is to *Make it hard to say no.*

The Breakthrough Strategy

This book lays out a five-step strategy for meeting these challenges—the strategy of breakthrough negotiation. Taken in sequence, the five steps enable you to change the game from face-to-face confrontation to side-by-side problem-solving. While no method can guarantee success, the breakthrough strategy will maximize your chances of getting what you need in even the toughest negotiations.

The breakthrough strategy is counterintuitive: It requires you to do the opposite of what you might naturally do in difficult situations. When your opponent stonewalls or attacks you, you feel like responding in kind. When he insists on his position, you want to reject it and assert your own. When he exerts pressure, you are inclined to retaliate with direct counterpressure. But in trying to break down your opponent's resistance, you usually only increase it.

The essence of the breakthrough strategy is indirect action. You try to *go around* his resistance. Rather than pounding in a new idea from the outside, you encourage him to reach for it from within. Rather than telling him what to do, you let him figure it out. Rather than trying to break down his resistance, you make it easier for him to break through it himself. In short, breakthrough negotiation is the art of letting the other person have *your* way.

Breakthrough negotiation can be used with any opponent—with an irascible boss, a temperamental teenager, a hostile co-worker, or an impossible customer. It can be used by diplomats trying to stave off a war, lawyers trying to avoid a costly court battle, or spouses trying to keep a marriage together. It is an all-purpose strategy that anyone can use.

STEP ONE

Don't React

GO TO THE BALCONY

Speak when you are angry and you will make the best speech you will ever regret.

—AMBROSE BIERCE

If you watch the negotiations going on around you, you will see countless instances in which people react to each other without thinking. Too many negotiations proceed like this:

HUSBAND *(thinking he is focused on the problem):* Honey, we've got to do something about the house. It's a mess.

WIFE *(perceiving this as a personal attack):* You don't lift a finger! You don't even do the things you promise. Last night—

HUSBAND *(interrupting):* I know. I know. It's just that—

WIFE *(not listening):* —you said you'd take out the garbage. I had to do it this morning.

HUSBAND *(trying to return to the problem):* Don't get defensive. I was just trying to point out that we're both—

WIFE *(not listening):* And it was your turn to take the kids to school.

HUSBAND *(reacting):* Come on! I told you I had a breakfast meeting this morning.

WIFE *(beginning to shout):* Oh, so your time is more important than mine, is it? I have a job too! I'm sick and tired of playing second fiddle in this band.

HUSBAND *(beginning to shout):* Give me a break! Who's paying most of the bills around here?

Neither the husband's interest in a clean house nor the wife's interest in more help is advanced by this exchange. But that doesn't stop either spouse from going at the other. Action provokes reaction, reaction provokes counterreaction, and on it goes in an endless argument. The same pattern repeats itself when business partners quarrel about who gets the corner office, when union and management officials wrestle over work rules, or when ethnic groups battle over territory.

Three Natural Reactions

Human beings are reaction machines. The most natural thing to do when confronted with a difficult situation is to react—to act without thinking. There are three common reactions:

Strike Back

When someone attacks you, your instinctive reaction is to attack right back, to "fight fire with fire" and "give him a taste of his own medicine." If he takes a rigid and extreme position, you do the same.

Occasionally, this will show your opponent that two can play the same game and will make him stop. More often, however, this strategy will land you in a futile and costly confrontation. You will provide him with a justification for his unreasonable behavior. He will say to himself: "Ah, I knew that you were out to get me. This proves it." Escalation often follows in the form of a shouting match, a corporate showdown, a lawsuit, or a war.

Take the example of the senior manager who had developed a new information system for his company's manufacturing process. To implement it he needed the agreement of all the plant managers across the country. Everyone agreed except for the manager of the largest plant in Dallas, who told him: "I don't want your people fooling around in my business. The only way things get done around here is if I'm in control. I can do the job better on my own." Frustrated, the systems manager reacted by threatening to take the matter to the company president, but that only enraged the plant manager. The end result: the systems manager's appeal to the company president backfired, since it implied the manager couldn't work smoothly with his peers. What's more, the president refused to intervene, and the new information system languished on the drawing table.

Striking back rarely advances your immediate interests and usually damages your long-term relationships. Even if you do win the battle, you may lose the war.

The other problem with striking back is that people who play hardball are usually very good at it. They may actually be hoping that you are going to attack them. If you do, you put yourself on their home turf, playing the game the way they like to play it.

Give In

The opposite of striking back is giving in. Your opponent may succeed in making you feel so uncomfortable with the negotiation that you give in just to be done with it. He pressures you, implying that you are the one who is blocking agreement. Do you really want to be the one responsible for dragging out the negotiations, disrupting the relationship, missing the opportunity of a lifetime? Wouldn't it just be better to say yes?

Many of us make agreements only to wake up the next

morning slapping our foreheads and exclaiming, "How could I have been so stupid! What did I agree to?" Many of us sign contracts—for example, when buying a car—without reading all the fine print. Why? Because the salesperson is leaning over us, the kids are eagerly waiting to drive home in the new car, and we're afraid of looking stupid if we ask questions about the contract, which is totally incomprehensible anyway.

Giving in usually results in an unsatisfactory outcome. You feel "had." Moreover, it rewards your opponent for bad behavior and gives you a reputation for weakness that he—and others—may try to exploit in the future. Just as giving in to a child's temper tantrum only reinforces this behavior pattern, so, too, giving in to an angry person only encourages angry outbursts in the future. Your boss's or client's terrible temper may appear to be uncontrollable—but a temper *can* be controlled. He probably doesn't throw a tantrum in front of *his* boss.

Sometimes we are intimidated and appease an unreasonable person under the illusion that if we give in just this one last time, we will get him off our back and will never have to deal with him again. All too often, however, that person comes back for further concessions. There is a saying that an appeaser is someone who believes that if you keep on throwing steaks to a tiger, the tiger will eventually become a vegetarian.

Break Off

A third common reaction is to break off relations with the difficult person or organization. If it's a marriage, get a divorce. If it's a job, resign. If you are involved in a joint venture, dissolve it.

At times, avoidance is a perfectly appropriate strategy.

Sometimes it is better to end a personal or business relationship if continuing means being taken advantage of or getting into fights again and again. Sometimes, too, breaking off reminds your opponent of the stake he has in the relationship and leads him to act more reasonably.

But the costs—both financial and emotional—of breaking off the relationship are often high: a lost client, a career setback, a shattered family. Breaking off is frequently a hasty reaction that we come to regret later. We all know people who take a job or enter a personal relationship, become frustrated with their boss or partner, and then leave without giving it a chance. Often they misinterpret the other person's behavior and do not try to work it out. A pattern of breaking off relationships means you never get anywhere because you are always starting over.

The Dangers of Reacting

In reacting, we lose sight of our interests. Consider the Pentagon's reaction to the Iranian hostage crisis of 1979–1981. Shortly after the crisis began, a news reporter asked a Pentagon spokesperson what the armed forces were doing to help. The spokesperson answered that there was not much they could do without jeopardizing the lives of the American hostages. The Pentagon, he continued, was working on tough measures to be carried out *after* the hostages were released. But he wasn't thinking clearly: Why would the Iranian students release the hostages if they believed that the United States would retaliate soon afterward? The Pentagon made the all-too-common mistake of confusing getting even with getting what you want.

Often your opponent is actually trying to make you react. The first casualty of an attack is your objectivity—the faculty you need most to negotiate effectively. Your opponent is trying to throw you off balance and prevent you from thinking straight. He is trying to bait you like a fish so that he can control you. When you react, you are hooked.

Much of your opponent's power lies in his ability to make you react. Have you ever wondered how a small terrorist group in the Middle East can command worldwide attention and create sleepless nights for the leader of the most powerful nation on earth—simply by nabbing a passing American on the street? The hostage-takers have hardly any power in and of themselves—their power comes from the reaction of the American public.

Even if reacting doesn't lead to a gross error on your part, it feeds the unproductive cycle of action and reaction. Ask the wife why she shouts at her husband and she may answer, "Because *he* shouts at me." Ask the husband and he will give the same answer: "Because *she* shouts at me." By reacting, you become part of the problem. Just as it takes two to tango, it takes two to tangle.

Go to the Balcony

If the bad news is that you contribute to the vicious cycle of action and reaction, the good news is that you have the power to break the cycle at any time—*unilaterally*. How? By *not* reacting. In physics class we learn that "for every action, there is an equal and opposite reaction." Newton's law, however, applies to objects, not minds. *Objects react. Minds can choose not to.*

O. Henry's story "The Ransom of Red Chief" offers a fictional example of the power of not reacting. When their son was kidnapped, the parents chose not to respond to the kidnappers' demands. As time passed, the boy became such a burden to the kidnappers that they offered to pay the parents to take him back. The story illustrates the psychological game that depends on your reacting. By refusing to react, the parents thwarted the kidnappers' plans.

When you find yourself facing a difficult negotiation, you need to step back, collect your wits, and see the situation objectively. Imagine you are negotiating on a stage and then imagine yourself climbing onto a balcony overlooking the stage. The "balcony" is a metaphor for a mental attitude of detachment. From the balcony you can calmly evaluate the conflict, almost as if you were a third party. You can think constructively for both sides and look for a mutually satisfactory way to resolve the problem.

In the ancient Japanese art of swordsmanship, students were instructed to look at an opponent as if he were a far-off mountain. Musashi, the greatest samurai of all, called this a "distanced view of close things." Such is the view from the balcony.

Going to the balcony means distancing yourself from your natural impulses and emotions. Consider the case of a film executive named Janet Jenkins, who was winding up a multimillion-dollar sale of programming to a cable TV network. An hour into her final meeting with the network negotiator, the head of the network stormed in. He attacked Janet's product and her personal integrity and demanded radical changes in the deal. Instead of reacting, however, Janet controlled her emotions and went to her mental balcony. She realized that defending herself or counterattacking would only add fuel to the fire and would not bring her any closer to clinching the deal. So she simply heard the network chairman out. After he finished and left the room, Janet excused herself for a minute, ostensibly to make a phone call but actually to recover her mental balance.

When she returned, the network negotiator looked up and asked, "Now, shall we pick up our conversation where *we* left off?" He was saying, in other words: "Discount what the chairman said. He was just blowing off steam. Let's get back to business." If Janet had reacted, the negotiation would have gone way off course. Because she had gone to the balcony instead, she was able to proceed smoothly to conclude the deal.

You ought to go to the balcony before the negotiation even begins—in order to prepare. And you should go to the balcony at every possible opportunity throughout the negotiation. At all times, you will be tempted to react impulsively to your opponent's difficult behavior. But at all times, you need to remember what you are after.

Keep Your Eyes on the Prize

The prize in negotiation is *not* obtaining your position, but satisfying your interests. The distinction is fundamental. On the balcony, the first thing you need to do is figure out your interests.

Identify Your Interests

When you ask yourself what you want, your answer is usually concrete: "I want my boss to approve a twelve percent increase in my department's budget for next year." This is your *position*, the concrete things you say you want—the terms and conditions, the dollars and cents. Behind your position lie your *interests*. Your interests are the intangible motivations that lead you to take that position: your needs, desires, concerns, and fears. Your interest in wanting the budget increase may be to buy computers to boost your department's productivity. You uncover your interests by asking the simple question *Why?* "Why do I want that? What problem am I trying to solve?"

Negotiation, however, is a two-way street. You usually can't satisfy your interests unless you also satisfy your opponent's. It is therefore just as important to understand his interests as your own. Your boss's reluctance to give you the budget increase may stem from his interest in becoming company president, which he thinks depends on the board's perception that he runs a tight ship.

While it may not be possible to obtain your position, it is often possible to satisfy your interests. You may not succeed in winning the twelve percent budget increase, but you may invent an option that allows you to computerize your department while making your boss look good to the board. Could you implement your plan in stages so that you would need only a six percent increase this year with a promise of six percent next year after the board has picked the next president? Could your boss help you get free in-house technical assistance to cut your costs? Or could he obtain extra funds from a separate capital budget? Many options may come to mind *after* you have identified your underlying interests.

Don't think of your options as rigid objectives; consider them as concrete illustrations of the kind of outcomes that would satisfy your interests. The prize would be an agreement *like* that. You cannot know for certain that the other person will agree to your idea. And you may learn something in the course of the negotiation that will enable you to come up with an even better option.

Identify Your BATNA

The prize is not just an agreement that satisfies your interests minimally; the agreement must satisfy your interests *better* than you could by pursuing your BATNA.

Your BATNA is your Best Alternative To a Negotiated Agreement. It is your best way of satisfying your interests *without* the other's agreement. If you are negotiating with your boss over a raise, your BATNA might be to find a job with another firm. If you are negotiating with your teenager over his or her messy room, your BATNA may be to clean up the room yourself. Clearly, these alternatives entail costs to you and to the relationship, which is why you are negotiating to develop a better solution. Your BATNA should be your measuring stick for evaluating any potential agreement.

To identify your BATNA, you should consider three kinds of alternatives. First, what can you do all by yourself to pursue your interests? Your "walkaway alternative" may be to find another supplier if you're a buyer, or another customer if you're a seller. Second, what can you do directly to your opponent to make him respect your interests? Your "interactive alternative" may be to go on strike or to go to war. Third, how can you bring a third party into the situation to further your interests? Your "third-party alternative" may be to go to court or to arbitration. After generating a set of possibilities, select the best.

A good BATNA usually does not already exist; it needs to be developed. If your BATNA is not very strong, you should take steps to improve it. For instance, don't just identify your BATNA as seeking another job in the same industry. Go to the trouble of getting an actual job offer. If you are selling your house, don't stop showing it just because someone is interested; try to line up another potential buyer.

BATNA is the key to negotiating power. Your power depends less on whether you are bigger, stronger, more senior, or richer than your opponent than on how good your BATNA is. The better your other job offer, the more likely you are to get a satisfactory raise, especially if your boss doesn't have someone else in mind for your job. If you have a viable alternative and your opponent does not, then you have leverage in the negotiation. The better your BATNA, the more power you have.

Keep your BATNA in your back pocket. When you're under heavy attack and feel panicky, you can pat your back pocket and say to yourself, "I'm okay if it doesn't go okay."

Decide if You Should Negotiate

Now that you know your interests and have considered your BATNA, you should ask yourself whether you should negotiate at all. Have you ever wondered why some people keep trying to negotiate with an abusive boss long after they should have left the job? Habit, guilt, self-blame, and fear may all play a role, but often the employee has failed to identify or has lost sight of his best alternative.

Perhaps your BATNA *is* better than any agreement you could reach with your opponent. Remember, too, that the negotiation process itself is not free of costs. It can take a lot of time and effort, in the course of which your other alternatives may vanish. Your decision to negotiate should therefore be a carefully considered one.

Keep in mind that it is easy to overestimate how good your BATNA is. Many business executives, listening to the advice of overconfident lawyers, have eschewed negotiations and taken a dispute to court, only to find themselves on the path to financial ruin. In any lawsuit, strike, or war, one contender—and often two—discovers that his BATNA wasn't as good as he imagined. Knowing in advance that your alternative is unattractive ought to motivate you to make a strong effort to reach agreement.

Stay Focused on Your Goal

The prize, therefore, is an agreement that satisfies your interests, certainly better than your BATNA could. It must also meet your opponent's interests acceptably. Once you have an idea of what the prize looks like, your challenge is to stay focused on obtaining it. This is not easy. When you feel angry and defensive, you feel like striking out. When you're frustrated and fearful, you feel like walking away. How can you suspend your natural reaction?

Name the Game

Often you don't even realize you are reacting, because you are too enmeshed in the situation. The first task, therefore, is to recognize the tactic. In ancient mythology, calling an evil spirit by its name enabled you to ward it off. So, too, with unfair tactics—identify them and you break the spell they cast.

Three Kinds of Tactics

There are dozens of tactics, but they can be grouped into three general categories, depending on whether they are obstructive, offensive, or deceptive:

Stone walls. A stone-wall tactic is a refusal to budge. Your opponent tries to convince you that he has no flexibility and that there is no choice other than his position. Stone walls can take the form of a *fait accompli:* "What's done is done. It can't be changed." Or a resort to company policy: "I can't do anything about it. It's company policy." Or a reference to a previous commitment: "I told the membership that I would resign as union negotiator before I would accept less than an eight percent raise." Your opponent may engage in endless foot-dragging and delay: "We'll get back to you." Or he may issue a final declaration: "You can take it or leave it!" Any other suggestion on your part is met with a no.

Attacks. Attacks are pressure tactics designed to intimidate you and make you feel so uncomfortable that you ultimately give in to your opponent's demands. Perhaps the most common form of attack is to threaten you with dire consequences unless you accept his position: "Do it *or else!*" Your opponent may also attack your proposal ("Your figures are way out of line!"), your credibility ("You haven't been in this job long, have you?"), or your status and authority ("We want to talk to the *real* decision maker."). An attacker will insult, badger, and bully until he gets his way.

Tricks. Tricks are tactics that dupe you into giving in. They take advantage of the fact that you assume your counterpart is acting in good faith and is telling the truth. One kind of trick is manipulating the data—using false, phony, or confusing figures. Another is the "no authority" ploy, in which your opponent misleads you into believing he has the authority to decide the issue, only to inform you after you have given up as much as you can that in fact someone else must decide. A third trick is the "add on," the last-minute additional demand that comes after your opponent has led you to believe you have already reached agreement.

Step 1. Don't React

Recognize the Tactic

The key to neutralizing a tactic's effect on you is to recognize it. If you recognize your opponent's tactic as a stone wall, you are less likely to assume that your opponent is inflexible. If you recognize an attack, you are less likely to fall prey to fear and discomfort. If you recognize a trick, you will not be taken in by the deception.

Consider an example. Mr. and Mrs. Albin had just sold their house—or at least that is what they thought they had done as they packed up all their belongings and prepared to move. Then the buyer, Mr. Maloney, demanded that the closing be postponed four months because he could not sell his own house. He refused to compensate the Albins for the delay. They in turn told him they would have to look for another buyer. Mr. Maloney responded, "You know, you're lucky you're dealing with someone like me. Other people I know would sue to prevent you from selling to anyone else. Your property could be tied up in court for years! But since we're practically friends by now, I'm sure we can avoid all that."

When Mr. Maloney left, Mr. Albin let out a sigh of relief and told his wife: "Thank God he's not going to sue. We would have been stuck in this place for years. Maybe we should accommodate him a little." Whereupon Mrs. Albin replied, "Honey, you've just been threatened in a nice way, and you don't even realize it. He *is* the type who'd sue, and we need to deal with him accordingly." Mr. Albin reacted to Mr. Maloney's tactic with fear—just as Mr. Maloney intended. In contrast, Mrs. Albin controlled her reaction by naming the game.

Many ploys depend on your not knowing what is being done to you. Suppose your customer tells you that he loves the deal but that his partner won't let him sign the contract without substantial changes. If you don't realize that he is using his partner as a "bad guy," you may agree innocently to the changes. Recognizing the tactic, however, puts you on your guard.

The hardest tactics to recognize are lies. Your opponent is trying his best to persuade you that he is telling you the truth when he isn't. You need to watch for *mismatch*—between his words, on the one hand, and his previous words or actions, facial expressions, body language, and tone of voice, on the other. Whereas a liar can manipulate his words, he cannot easily control the anxiety that raises his voice pitch. Nor can he control the symmetry of his facial expressions; his smile, for instance, may become crooked. Bear in mind that anxiety can stem from other causes and that one clue alone is unreliable. You need to look for multiple clues.

Watching out for tactics means being alert, not overly suspicious. Sometimes you may have misunderstood the other person's behavior. One of the most celebrated political images in modern times is that of Soviet Premier Nikita Khrushchev pounding his shoe on the podium while delivering a speech at the United Nations in 1960. Everyone interpreted his histrionics as a tactic aimed at intimidating the West; a man who would pound his shoe one moment might use his nuclear weapons the next! Thirty years later, Khrushchev's son Sergei explained his father had had something far different in mind. Khrushchev, who had rarely been outside the Soviet Union, had heard that people in the West loved passionate political debate. So he gave his audience what he thought they wanted—he pounded his shoe to make his point. When people were shocked, no one was more surprised than Khrushchev himself. He had just been trying to look like one of the guys. What became the very image of the irrational Russian was apparently the result of a simple cross-cultural misunderstanding.

So put on your radar, not your armor. Make a mental note when you detect a possible trick or subtle attack. Neutralize it by naming it, and keep it in mind as a possibility, not a certainty. Look for additional evidence, remembering that difficult people rarely limit themselves to a single tactic.

Know Your Hot Buttons

To properly neutralize the effect of your opponent's tactic on you, you need to recognize not only what he is doing but also what you're feeling.

The first clue that you are reacting usually comes from your body. Your stomach gets tied up in knots. Your heart starts to pound. Your face flushes. Your palms sweat. These are all visceral responses signaling that something is wrong and that you are losing your composure in the negotiation. They are cues that you need to go to the balcony.

Each of us has certain emotional susceptibilities, or "hot buttons." Some of us react bitterly to even minor criticism, or see red when we think someone is making fun of us. Some of us can't stand to have our ideas rejected. Others of us give in because we feel guilty, or because we are worried people won't like us, or because we don't want to cause a scene.

If you understand what your "hot buttons" are, you can more easily recognize when your opponent is pushing them. Recognizing them in turn allows you to control your natural reaction. If you hate being called disorganized, and you *know* you hate it, you can prepare yourself to deal with it. When someone calls you chaotic, you can simply shrug it off.

We live and work in competitive environments. So expect

verbal attacks and don't take them personally. Remember that your accuser is hoping to play on your anger, fear, and guilt. He may want you to lose control of your emotions so that you cannot negotiate effectively. As children we learned when a playmate insulted us to say: "Sticks and stones may break my bones, but words will never hurt me." It is a simple lesson we would do well to remember as adults.

When you are being attacked, it may help to see your opponent as someone who doesn't know any better. Consider the approach taken by a woman whose boss periodically savaged her in front of her peers: "I was carrying him home in my head, driving myself and my family crazy. . . . But then I decided he wasn't my life. I began to detach myself and say, 'Poor guy, he doesn't know a better way to behave.' " No matter what he did, she wouldn't react: "He saw that he wasn't getting to me, and his bullying behavior began to subside."

Buy Time to Think

Once you have named the game and forestalled your immediate reaction, the next step is to buy yourself time to think —time to go to the balcony.

Pause and Say Nothing

The simplest way to buy time to think in the middle of a tense negotiation is to pause and say nothing. It does you little good to respond when you're feeling angry or frustrated. Your judgment is distorted. This is not simply a psychological fact; it results from actual biochemical changes associated with anger and stress. Even taking a few seconds for these changes to dissipate will allow you to see things more objectively. Hence the wisdom of pausing before you reply. As Thomas Jefferson once put it: "When angry, count ten before you speak; if *very* angry, a hundred."

Pausing will not only give you a chance to step up to the balcony for a few seconds, but it may also help your opponent to cool down. By saying nothing you give him nothing to push against. Your silence may make him feel a little uncomfortable. The onus of keeping the conversation going shifts back to him. Uncertain about what is going on in your head, he may respond more reasonably. Some of the most effective negotiation is accomplished by saying nothing.

Suppose, however, that your opponent continues to rage. A movie producer, for instance, had a boss who used to blow up over the most trivial matters. The producer told a friend that he felt like punching his boss in the nose. The friend counseled, "Think about it this way. He's not yelling *at* you, he's yelling *for* himself. Next time he shouts at you, this is what you do. You lean back in your chair, fold your arms, and let his screams wash over you. Tell yourself how much good it's doing him to get it out of his system." The movie producer reported later that the plan worked wonders.

The same approach has been used to head off the verbal battles that so often erupt in labor-management negotiations. In one case both sides adopted a ground rule that "only one person can get angry at a time." The other side was obliged not to react; to do so would be an admission that they were weak and could not control themselves. The rule helped break the escalating cycle of action and reaction.

You obviously can't eliminate your feelings, nor do you

need to do so. You need only to disconnect the automatic link between emotion and action. Feel the anger, frustration, or fear—even imagine attacking your opponent if you like—but *don't* channel your feelings and impulses into action. Suspend your impulses; freeze your behavior. While it may feel like hours, it will probably last only a few seconds. This may not be easy when your opponent is shouting or stonewalling, but it is necessary for successful negotiation. Follow the biblical dictum: "Be quick to hear, slow to speak, and slow to act."

Rewind the Tape

You can pause for only so long. To buy more time to think, try rewinding the tape. Slow down the conversation by playing it back. Tell your counterpart: "Let me just make sure I understand what you're saying." Review the discussion up to that point.

Suppose you have just concluded a sale and you are going over the contract with the customer. "I think we have a terrific package here," he says, "and I'd be willing to go ahead if you will throw in the service contract, you know, gratis. What do you say? Can we call it a deal?" The customer extends his hand.

If you react to the trick and decide yes or no on the spot, there is a good chance you will make the wrong decision. To give yourself time on the balcony, rewind the tape. Look the customer in the eye and say, "Hold on, Larry. I'm not sure I'm following you. Let's back up for a minute and review how we got here. We started discussing this deal three months ago, back in March, right?"

"I guess so," Larry says.

"At the start I thought you said you wanted to negotiate the service contract separately from the purchase."

"Yes, but I've changed my mind on that."

"Larry, correct me if I'm wrong, but didn't you and I reach final agreement on all the clauses the day before yesterday?"

Whichever way Larry responds at this point, you are on the balcony, no longer reacting to his last-minute demand. You have not fallen for the trick. In fact, you have now caused Larry to shift from being on the offensive to being slightly on the defensive.

Tactics such as Larry's are like magic tricks; they are done so quickly you often don't see the sleight of hand. By rewinding the tape—which interrupts the routine and slows it down—you give yourself time to recognize the trick and neutralize its impact.

If your opponent overloads you with information, hoping you will overlook a hidden drawback in his proposal, don't hesitate to say "You've given me too much information to digest so quickly. Let's back up." Or "I need you to tell me again how the different components of your plan work together. I missed the connections between a couple of them." By asking him to give a detailed account, you can more easily spot the flaws in his logic.

An easy way to slow down the negotiation is to take careful notes. Writing down what your opponent says gives you a good excuse: "I'm sorry, I missed that. Could you please repeat it?" Keeping a record not only buys you time to think, but also shows that you are taking the other person seriously.

Some people are afraid they will appear stupid if they say "I'm not sure I'm following you." Ironically, they are the ones most likely to be taken in, because they don't ask the questions they ought to ask. Successful negotiators learn that appearing a little obtuse can be a negotiating advantage. It allows you to slow down the discussion. You need not pretend to be stupid. Simply ask for some clarification: "I'm afraid I don't understand why you waited until now to ask for a discount."

If you can't think of anything else to say on the spot, you can always resort to the rote phrase "Let me make sure I understand what you're saying."

Take a Time-out

If you need more time to think, you should take a break. Too many negotiations go on and on as each person reacts to the other's provocations. A time-out gives both sides a chance to cool off and go to the balcony. Negotiations are more productive when they are broken up by frequent time-outs.

You might be afraid that calling for a break will be interpreted as a sign of indecisiveness or weakness, as if you couldn't take the heat. The solution is to find a natural excuse. Such an excuse may be as simple as "We've been talking for some time now. Before continuing, let me suggest a quick coffee break." Or "That's a good question. Let me find out and get back to you right away." It helps to have a ready excuse.

One of the best excuses is to call a caucus with your negotiating team. You might be worried about looking conspiratorial, but calling a caucus is perfectly legitimate; your opponent has just offered new information or made a new proposal, and you need a chance to discuss it among yourselves. If you are buying a car, tell the high-pressure salesperson: "My wife and I would like a moment to think about the decision. We're going to go for a walk around the block. We'll be back in half an hour." If you are negotiating by yourself, caucus on the phone with a colleague, boss, or friend.

If you can't leave the room, try to take a time-out from the negotiation by temporarily diverting the conversation with a story or joke. One union negotiator keeps snapshots of his fishing trips in his pocket and tosses them on the table when things get tense. All the participants start talking about their own adventures. When negotiations resume, tensions have abated.

Another way to take time out during the negotiation is to bring along a negotiating partner. That way you can spell each other; as one person talks, the other can go to the balcony and keep his eyes on the prize. Police negotiators dealing with a hostage-taker routinely work with a partner who gives them unbiased and realistic feedback on how they're doing, makes sure they don't become reactive, and relieves them when they get tired.

Don't Make Important Decisions on the Spot

In the presence of your opponent, you are under strong psychological pressure to agree. One simple rule of thumb will help keep you out of trouble: Never make an important decision on the spot. Go to the balcony and make it there.

If your opponent springs a contract on you and demands an immediate signature, say: "My lawyer insists on checking everything over. You know how lawyers are." Or ask: "You've put a lot of time and thought into this, haven't you?" As he nods his head, continue: "In that case, I'd like to do it justice by studying it carefully before responding." Fold up the document and put it away, saying: "I'll get back to you tomorrow."

While it is generally better to sleep on a prospective decision, it isn't always possible. If an immediate response is required, tell your opponent: "I don't want to slow things down. Let me make a quick phone call to my office, and I'll get right back to you. If you'll excuse me, I'll make that call right now." Even if you have time only to step out into the corridor for a moment, it will help. Once you are away from the table, the psychological pressure eases. It no longer seems so urgent to reach a decision. Having suspended your initial reaction, you can now consider the decision in a more objective fashion—on the balcony.

Don't let yourself be hurried. If your opponent sets a deadline, don't hesitate to test it by adjourning the meeting. If he is serious about the deadline, he will let you know. Remember that agreement requires your assent. Your worst enemy is your own quick reaction; only *you* can make the concession you will later regret.

Don't Get Mad, Don't Get Even, Get What You Want

In sum, the most natural thing to do when faced with a difficult person or situation is to react. It is also the biggest mistake you can make.

The first thing you need to do in dealing with a difficult person is not to control his behavior but to control your own. Suspend your natural reaction by naming the game. Then buy yourself time to think. Use the time to keep your eyes on the prize—an agreement that satisfies your interests, certainly better than your BATNA can. Instead of getting mad or getting even, concentrate on getting what you want. That is what going to the balcony is all about.

STEP TWO

Disarm Them

STEP TO THEIR SIDE

> Rarely is it advisable to meet prejudices and passions head on. Instead, it is best to appear to conform to them in order to gain time to combat them. One must know how to sail with a contrary wind and to tack until one meets a wind in the right direction.
> —FORTUNE DE FELICE, 1778

An AT&T sales team was negotiating to sell Boeing a new telecommunications system valued at $150 million. The sales team made a persuasive pitch on the kind of service to be delivered, the company's prompt response to problems, and the speed of repairs.

Then the Boeing purchasing director said, "Fine. Now put each one of your promises in writing. And we want guarantees that if the system isn't fixed on time, you'll pay us damages."

"We'll make our best efforts," replied the AT&T sales chief, "but we can't be held liable for all the things that can go wrong. Lightning can strike—"

"You're fooling around with us!" interrupted the Boeing negotiator, losing his temper. "First you tell us about your services—now you're not willing to commit yourself to what you promised!"

"That's not true!" protested the sales chief, aghast at the turn in the negotiation. "Let me see if I can explain—"

But the Boeing negotiator refused to listen. "You're not negotiating in good faith!" he complained. "We can't deal with you."

The AT&T sales chief made a last-ditch effort: "Let's talk about it. Maybe we can put some of it in writing." But the Boeing purchasing director had already made up his mind. He and his team walked out the door.

What happened? When AT&T refused to go along with Boeing's demand, the Boeing negotiator got angry and went on the attack. The AT&T sales chief defended himself, but this just fueled the buyer's anger. When the sales chief tried to explain, the buyer wouldn't listen. Nothing seemed to work.

The mistake, a common one, is in trying to reason with a person who is not receptive. Your words will fall on deaf ears or be misconstrued. Before you can discuss the *problem,* you need to disarm the *person.* Going to the balcony has enabled you to regain your mental balance. Now you need to help your opponent regain his.

Like the Boeing negotiator, your opponent may feel distrustful, angry, or threatened. Convinced he is right and you are wrong, he may be unwilling to listen. Disarming him means defusing his hostile emotions. It means getting him to hear your point of view. And it means garnering a measure of his respect. He doesn't need to like you, but he does need to take you seriously and treat you as a human being.

The secret of disarming is surprise. To disarm your opponent, you need to do the opposite of what he expects. If he is stonewalling, he expects you to apply pressure; if he is attacking, he expects you to resist. So don't pressure; don't resist. Do the opposite: Step to his side. Listen to him, acknowledge his point, and agree wherever you can.

Stepping to his side is probably the last thing you feel like doing with a difficult person. When your opponent closes his ears, you naturally feel like doing the same. When he refuses to recognize your point of view, you certainly don't feel like recognizing his. When he disagrees with everything you say, you may find it difficult to agree with *anything* he says. Although entirely understandable, this tit-for-tat response is a recipe for stalemate.

To break through your opponent's resistance, you need to reverse this dynamic. If you want him to listen to you, begin by listening to him. If you want him to acknowledge your point, acknowledge his first. To get him to agree with you, begin by agreeing with him wherever you can.

Listen Actively

Too often negotiations proceed as follows: Party A sets out his opening position. Party B is so focused on figuring out what he will say that he doesn't really listen. When Party B's turn comes to lay out *his* position, Party A thinks, "He didn't respond to what I said. He must not have heard me. I'd better repeat it." Then Party B concludes that he, too, has not been properly heard, so he repeats his position. And on it goes—in a dialogue of the deaf. "Everything has been said before," says a character in a novel by André Gide, "but since nobody listens, we have to keep going back and beginning all over again."

You have an opportunity to interrupt the chorus of monologues if you are willing to be the first to listen.

Give Your Opponent a Hearing

Listening to someone may be the cheapest concession you can make. We all feel a deep need to be understood. By satisfying that need, you can help turn the negotiation around.

Consider a contract negotiation between union and management at an Inland Steel container plant. The corporate counsel took a rigid position on the crucial issue of wage arbitration, saying, "Now *that* is one I believe we're going to have to *insist* on." The general manager, Robert Novy, added, "That is putting it pretty mildly."

Normally the union would have counterattacked, management would have vehemently defended its position, and after a futile argument a strike would have ensued. Indeed, the previous breakdown in negotiations had resulted in a mutually disastrous 191-day strike, and everyone expected a strike this time too. But instead of counterattacking, chief union negotiator Jake Shafer said quietly, "I am interested in Mr. Novy's statement. You say, 'That is putting it pretty mildly.' "

With this invitation, Novy went on to explain at length why management felt so strongly about the issue. Having received the satisfaction of a full hearing, management in turn gave the union a hearing of *its* concerns. It may have seemed at the time like a small tactical move, but Shafer's decision to sit back and ask management to discuss its point of view broke open the deadlocked issue for eventual resolution. The strike that everyone expected never materialized.

Listening requires patience and self-discipline. Instead of reacting immediately or plotting your next step, you have to remain focused on what your counterpart is saying. Listening may not be an easy thing to do, but, as the story of Inland Steel demonstrates, it can be enormously valuable. It offers a window into your opponent's mind. It gives you a chance to engage him in a cooperative task—that of understanding *his* problem. And it makes him more willing to listen to you.

If your opponent is angry or upset, the best thing you can offer is a full hearing of his grievance. Don't interrupt—even if you feel he is wrong or insulting. Let him know you're listening by maintaining eye contact, nodding occasionally, and responding with "Uh-huh" or "I see." When he winds down, ask quietly if there is anything more he would like to add. Encourage him to tell you everything that is bothering him by using such phrases as "Yes . . . please go on" and "Then what happened?"

People derive genuine satisfaction from voicing their feelings and resentments. Customer-service managers know that even if there is little they can do to help an angry, dissatisfied customer, giving him a full and respectful hearing can often be enough to keep him coming back.

Once you have heard your opponent out, he will most likely become less reactive, more rational, and more responsive to problem-solving negotiation. It is no coincidence that *effective negotiators listen far more than they talk.*

Paraphrase and Ask for Corrections

It is not enough for you to listen to your opponent. He needs to know that you've *heard* what he has said. So reflect back what you hear. A conversation between a salesperson and an unhappy customer might go this way:

CUSTOMER: I bought this answering machine from you barely six months ago, and now you can hardly hear the voices. It's not the tape—I replaced it. What kind of lousy machines do you sell here? I'm losing business because of you. I want it replaced right now with a quality machine, or this won't be the last you hear of me.

SALESPERSON: Okay, let me make sure I understand. You bought this machine here six months ago to use in your business. But now you can't hear the voices. You need a working machine, and time is of the essence. Have I got it right?

CUSTOMER: That's right.
SALESPERSON: Let's see what we can do for you.

Paraphrasing means summing up your understanding of what your opponent has said and repeating it back in your own words. Remember to retain *his* point of view. Adding your own or trying to make him see the error of his ways will not help. It will give the customer little satisfaction if you say "*You* couldn't make it work so you've brought it back?"

Paraphrasing gives your opponent the feeling of being understood as well as the satisfaction of correcting you. It gives you a chance to check and see whether you have gotten his message. Paraphrasing is one of the most useful techniques in a negotiator's repertoire.

Acknowledge the Point

After listening to your opponent, the next step is to acknowledge his point. You may be reluctant to do this because of your strong disagreement with him. But you thereby miss a critical opportunity. Every human being, no matter how impossible, has a deep need for recognition. By satisfying that need you can help create a climate for agreement.

Acknowledging your opponent's point does *not* mean that you agree with it. It means that you accept it as one valid point of view among others. It sends the message "I can see how you see things." It is conveyed in phrases such as "You have a point there" or "I know exactly what you mean" or "I understand what you're saying."

Your opponent's mind is often like a cluttered attic, full of old resentments and angers, gripes and stories. To argue with him just keeps all this stuff alive. But if you acknowledge the validity of what he says, it begins to lose its emotional charge. In effect, the stuff begins to disappear from the attic. By letting him tell his side of the story *and* acknowledging it, you create psychological room for him to accept that there may be another side of the story.

One of the most powerful and surprising ways to acknowledge your opponent's point is to preempt him. Take the words out of his mouth. Tell him: "If I were in your shoes, this is the way I'd see it." Former U.S. Defense Secretary Robert McNamara used this approach at a 1989 meeting of key American, Soviet, and Cuban participants in the 1962 Cuban missile crisis. Sensing that the Soviets and the Cubans were defensive about why their governments had decided to secretly install nuclear missiles in Cuba, he announced, "If *I* had been a Cuban or Soviet leader at the time, I would have concluded that the Americans intended to invade Cuba. From the evidence you had available to you, you were right to reach that conclusion. But I must tell you that we had no such intention." By preemptively acknowledging what the Soviets and Cubans were thinking, McNamara made them more receptive to hearing his viewpoint.

Acknowledge Your Opponent's Feelings

Don't ignore your opponent's emotions. Behind his attack often lies anger; behind his stonewalling often lies fear. Until you defuse his emotions, your reasonable arguments will fall on deaf ears.

Imagine that an employee storms into your office and rages, "I'm sick of being cheated! I just found out that Dayle Turner gets two thousand dollars more a year for doing the same job that I do. I'm through!"

Trying to explain why Dayle earns more money, even if the reason is a good one, may only make your employee angrier. Instead, you must acknowledge his feelings first. "You think we're taking advantage of you. I can understand that. I'd probably feel angry too."

This is not the response your employee expects. By acknowledging his feelings, you have helped him calm down.

He then asks, "Why shouldn't I make every penny as much as Dayle does? I do the same work!"

By asking you a question, albeit an angry one, he shows that he is ready to hear your explanation. Now you can proceed to reason with him.

Like the employee, your opponent often feels embattled and unappreciated. It is disarming to be met with an acknowledgment rather than an argument. Telling your opponent "I appreciate how you feel" or "If I were in your shoes, I'd be just as angry" lets him know his message has been heard and appreciated. Showing that you understand *why* he feels as he does enhances your acknowledgment.

One word of caution: your opponent will usually be able to tell whether or not your acknowledgment is sincere. Your intent, as expressed in your tone and body language, counts just as much as your words.

Offer an Apology

Perhaps the most powerful form of acknowledgment is an apology. This is a lesson we all learn as children. If you say the magic words "I'm sorry," you can continue playing the game. Unfortunately, it is a lesson we often forget as adults. Take the Columbia law professor who put the following question to his contracts class:

"Seller promises Buyer to deliver widgets at the rate of one thousand a month. The first two deliveries are perfect.

However, in the third month Seller delivers only nine hundred and ninety widgets. Buyer becomes so incensed that he rejects deliveries and refuses to pay for the widgets already delivered. If you were Seller, what would you say?"

The professor was looking for a discussion of the various common law theories that would, as he put it, "allow Seller to crush Buyer." He looked around the room for a volunteer, but found none. "As is so often the case with first-year students," he reported, "I found that they were all either writing in their notebooks or inspecting their shoes. There was, however, one eager face, that of an eight-year-old son of one of my students. He was in class because his mother couldn't find a sitter. Suddenly he raised his hand. Such behavior, even from an eight-year-old, must be rewarded.

" 'Okay,' I said, 'what would you say if you were the seller?'

" 'I'd say, "I'm sorry." ' "

As the child seemed to know instinctively, "crushing" an opponent is not the right answer. We often overlook the simple power of an apology. The buyer was outraged because he felt wronged. What such a person most often wants is the recognition that he *has* been wronged. Only when that acknowledgment has been made will he feel safe in negotiating. An apology thus creates the conditions for a constructive resolution of the dispute.

Your apology need not be meek, nor an act of self-blame. To a disgruntled customer, you could say, "I'm sorry you've had this problem. You're one of my favorite customers and the last person I'd want to see unhappy. What can we do to make it up to you?" Even if your opponent is primarily responsible for the mess you are in, consider apologizing for your share. Your bold gesture can set in motion a process of reconciliation in which he apologizes for *his* share.

Project Confidence

You may be afraid that acknowledging your opponent is an act of weakness. To the contrary, acknowledgment reflects your strength. To ensure that your opponent recognizes this, project confidence as you acknowledge him. In dealing with an attack, for example, put as reasonable an expression on your face as you can muster. Adopt a calm, confident posture and tone. Stand up straight, look your opponent in the eye, and use his name. Fearlessness disarms.

Consider how an American diplomat, held hostage in Iran from 1979 until 1981, took control by acknowledging his opponents. Whenever his guards came into his room, he would invite them to sit down. "They became *my* guests," explained the diplomat, "and in this small way, I established command of the situation. I created the unmistakable sense that this was *my* space, *my* territory, and it did wonders for my well-being."

Agree Wherever You Can

Once you have listened to your opponent and acknowledged what he has said, the next step is to agree wherever you can. It is hard to attack someone who agrees with you.

Agree Without Conceding

You don't need to concede a thing. Simply focus on issues on which you already agree. An American senator told his legislative staff: "Don't argue with my constituents, even if they're wrong. All you do is lose me votes. Do the *opposite* of what they taught you in graduate school. There, if someone said something you agreed with ninety-nine percent, you said, 'I disagree,' and you focused on the one percent of disagreement. Here, if my constituent says something you disagree with ninety-nine percent, I want you to say 'I agree with you' and focus on the one percent of agreement." It is natural to focus on differences, because differences cause the problem. At the outset, however, you are usually better off focusing on your common ground.

Look for any opportunity to agree—even if it is only in a humorous way. Humor has the added benefit of humanizing you in your opponent's eyes. Consider the example of a fund-raiser for the United Way who had to solicit contributions one day from a group of truck drivers as they showed up for work at six o'clock in the morning. At that hour no one had the slightest interest in United Way, but the boss had ordered the drivers to attend the meeting. As the fund-raiser was cheerily showing a videotape about the charity, the atmosphere in the room turned tense. When he passed out yellow pencils and pledge cards, the truck drivers stared at them and did nothing. Finally, one burly truck driver stood up, shook his pencil in a threatening fashion at the fund-raiser, and growled, "I'll tell you what you can do with this *pencil*!"

There was an awkward moment as everyone waited to see how the United Way representative would react. The fund-raiser looked the truck driver straight in the eye and said calmly, "Sir, I will be happy to do whatever you like with that pencil . . ." He paused, then added, ". . . *after* you sign the pledge card, of course." There was a brief moment of silence, and then one person started to laugh. Everyone joined in. The tension was broken. In the end, every truck driver signed a pledge card.

Accumulate Yeses

The key word in agreement is "yes." "Yes" is a magic word, a powerful tool for disarming your opponent. Look for occasions when you can say yes to the other side without making a concession. "Yes, you have a point there." "Yes, I agree with you." Say yes as often as possible.

You should also try to *get* as many yeses as you can. One public speaker uses this technique effectively to handle hostile comments from the audience. If someone says, "Your proposal is utterly unrealistic," he responds, "Are you saying you don't see how my budget proposal can possibly erase the deficit within five years—is that what you mean?" The audience member says yes, and as he does, the relationship between the speaker and the critic changes. The "yes" transforms an antagonistic argument into the beginning of a reasoned dialogue.

Each yes you elicit from your opponent further reduces tension. As you accumulate agreement, even if only on what he is saying, you create an atmosphere in which he is more likely to say yes to a substantive proposal.

Tune in to Your Opponent's Wavelength

Agreement can be nonverbal too. If you observe two friends deep in conversation, you will often notice something peculiar. If one friend leans on an elbow, the other does too. If one speaks in a low voice, the other lowers his voice. Almost unconsciously they align themselves with each other in order to communicate more effectively. Each is sending the other a subtle message: "I am like you."

Much of the message comes across in the form, not the content, of the communication. Observe your counterpart's communicative manner. If he speaks slowly, you may want to slow down your own speaking rate. If he talks softly, you may want to lower your voice. Observe his body posture too. If he leans forward to emphasize his point, consider leaning forward, too, to show your interest. Don't mimic. Just adapt your own communicative style to be more like his. Your goal is to tune in to the same wavelength.

It also pays to be sensitive to your opponent's language. If he is speaking in a colloquial fashion, you may want to make your language more colloquial. If he is from a different culture, it helps to learn and use a few polite phrases from *his* language in order to show your interest and respect.

People also use different "sensory languages," depending on whether they process information primarily through their eyes, ears, or feelings. If your opponent uses primarily visual terms, such as "Can't you *see* what I'm saying?" or "Let's *focus* on that," try to match him with similar phrases: "I do *see* your point" or "I can *picture* what you're saying." If your opponent uses primarily auditory terms, such as *"Listen* to this," respond with a phrase such as "I *hear* you." Or if his language is oriented around feelings, as in "That doesn't *feel* right to me," answer with phrases like, "I'm not *comfortable* either." Connect with your counterpart by using the language he understands best.

Acknowledge the Person

In listening to your opponent, acknowledging his point, and agreeing wherever you can, you are in fact acknowledging him as a person. You are showing him respect. Sometimes, however, you may want to acknowledge him in a more direct fashion.

Consider one of the world's most intractable disputes:

the Arab-Israeli conflict. Until 1977, Arab leaders refused to recognize Israel's existence; they would not even call it by its name. Then, in November of that year, Egyptian President Anwar Sadat broke the taboo with his dramatic journey to Jerusalem. Nothing could have been more surprising to the Israelis, more confusing to their perceptions of the Egyptians, or more disarming than the arrival of an enemy leader in the country his army had attacked a mere four years earlier. With this one action, he broke through the psychological barrier that constituted, in his words, ninety percent of the conflict. He created a climate that eventually produced a peace treaty between Egypt and Israel, which few had thought possible.

By acknowledging the person, you create what psychologists call "cognitive dissonance," an inconsistency between perception and reality. Your opponent thinks of you as an adversary. When you acknowledge him personally, you are acting as a friend or colleague, thus inducing him to change his perception of you in order to reduce the cognitive dissonance. Just as Sadat capitalized on the Israeli perception of him as a warmonger, you can capitalize on your opponent's negative perception of you by acting in a way that shatters his stereotype.

Reaffirming the person does not mean reaffirming his behavior. Parents continue to love their eight-year-old even after he puts glue between the newspaper pages and tries to strangle his younger sister. You need to distinguish between the person and his behavior.

Acknowledge His Authority and Competence

Suppose you are trying to persuade a difficult boss to change his mind about an office issue. He may perceive you to be personally challenging his authority or competence.

Are you implying, he wonders, that he is somehow incompetent or wrong? He will likely react by becoming even more resistant to what you have to say. To reassure him that you are not challenging him personally, you need to preface your remarks with a phrase such as "You're the boss" or "I respect your authority."

If your opponent has a big or vulnerable ego, think of it as an opportunity rather than an obstacle. A person whose ego needs stroking is dependent on the recognition of others. To the extent you can satisfy his need for recognition, you can disarm him. If you are seeking an exception to company policy from a self-important or insecure bureaucrat, you might begin by saying, "I've been told that you are the most knowledgeable person on this policy." To make your acknowledgment more credible, base it on facts. Instead of telling a departmental rival "You're the best salesperson around"—which he may dismiss as mere flattery—you might say, "Your presentation to the board was succinct, persuasive, and to the point. I don't think I've ever seen it done better."

Build a Working Relationship

One of the best ways to acknowledge your opponent is to build a working relationship. Invite him out for coffee or lunch, or meet for a drink after work. You can use such occasions to talk about hobbies and families, or whatever his interests are. Take time for small talk before the negotiation session begins and as it ends. Little gestures of goodwill can go a long way.

A good working relationship is like a savings account you can draw on in moments of trouble. When we deal with someone we know and like, we tend to attribute adverse events to extenuating circumstances: "Oh, I guess he didn't show up for the meeting because he was ill." When we deal with someone we don't like, we tend to attribute the same events to the person's basic nature: "He wants to keep me waiting to show me who has the upper hand." In short, if you have a positive relationship, your counterpart will be more inclined to give you the benefit of the doubt. You can thus prevent misunderstandings.

The best time to lay the foundation for a good relationship is *before* a problem arises. So if your job is likely to bring you into conflict with an individual, nurture the relationship from the earliest possible point. A production manager ought to have a healthy working relationship with his opposite number in marketing; a union chief, with his management counterpart; and a school principal, with the school board. When the other person is being difficult, you want to be able to say "Come on, Joe. We've always gotten on. We go back a long way."

Express Your Views— Without Provoking

Once you have heard and acknowledged your opponent, he is far more likely to listen to you. Now is the time to get *your* views across. You need to do so, however, without making him close his ears.

The secret lies in changing your mindset. The standard mindset is *either/or*. Either you are right or your opponent is. The alternative mindset is *both/and*. He can be right in terms of his experience, and you can be right in terms of yours. You can say to him: "I can see why you feel the way you do. It's entirely reasonable in terms of the experience you've had. My experience, however, has been different." You can acknowledge his view and, without challenging it, express a contrary one. You can create an inclusive atmosphere in which differences can coexist peacefully while you try to reconcile them.

Don't Say "But"; Say "Yes . . . And"

One of the most common methods of expressing your differences is to preface your views with the word "but." When your customer says "Your price is too high," you may be tempted to refute his statement with your own: *"But* this product is the highest quality you'll find!" Unfortunately, when your customer hears a "but," he may hear "I think you are wrong for the following reasons." Not surprisingly, he may stop listening.

Your opponent will be more receptive if you first acknowledge his views with a "yes" and then preface your own with an "and." After your customer complains about the high price, you could say, *"Yes,* you're absolutely correct that our price is higher. *And* what that increment buys you is higher quality, greater reliability, and better service!"

Even a direct disagreement can be framed inclusively: "I can see why you feel strongly about this, and I respect that. Let me tell you, however, how it looks from my angle," or "I am in total agreement with what you're trying to accomplish. What you may not have considered is . . ." Whatever language you use, the key is to present your views as an addition to, rather than a direct contradiction of, your opponent's point of view.

Make I-Statements, Not You-Statements

As you express your views, you will be less likely to provoke your counterpart if you speak about yourself, rather than about him. After all, your own experience is all you really know about anyway.

Suppose you are dealing with a difficult teenager who promised to come home by midnight but didn't show up until three o'clock in the morning. You could express your views by saying, "You broke your word! You're irresponsible." Or, "You only care about yourself. You never think about your family!" These are called "you-statements." The teenager naturally becomes defensive and angry. He tunes out the familiar parental lecture.

Suppose that you were to say instead: "Ken, I felt let down last night. I worried myself sick that something terrible had happened to you. I even called the highway patrol to see if you had been in an accident." Instead of attacking, you express your feelings and experience. These are "I-statements." The underlying message is the same, but phrased this way, your feelings are more likely to be heard.

The essence of an I-statement is to describe the impact of the problem on you. You are giving the other person information about the consequences of his behavior in a form that is hard for him to reject —because it is *your* experience. Common phrases to use are: "I feel . . . ," "I get upset when . . . , ' "I'm not comfortable with . . . ," and "The way I see it is . . ."

An I-statement does not challenge your opponent's views but simply offers him a different perspective—yours. It does not tell him what to do or how to think or how to feel. He is entitled to his opinions, and you are entitled to yours.

Note that just putting an "I" in front of a you-statement does not make it an I-statement. Telling your teenager "I feel that you have been irresponsible" or "I feel that you broke your word" is still accusatory and provokes the same defensive reaction. An I-statement focuses on *your* needs, concerns, feelings, and desires, not your opponent's short-comings.

Stand Up for Yourself

Don't hesitate to stand up for yourself. When threatened by the truck driver, the United Way fund raiser did more than just humorously acknowledge his demand. After saying "Sir, I will be happy to do whatever you like with that pencil," he added: *"after* you sign the pledge card, of course." He stood up for himself and his charity.

Standing up for yourself does not negate your acknowledgment. Acknowledgment from someone perceived as confident and strong is more powerful than acknowledgment from someone perceived as weak. The combination of seemingly opposite responses—acknowledging your opponent's views *and* expressing your own—is more effective than either alone.

Consider the parents faced with a bawling five-year-old who does not want to be left at home with a babysitter. Should they give in and stay home? Should they threaten to spank the child or try to appease him? A leading child psychologist suggests a third strategy. With empathy, tell the crying child: "I know you wish we were not going out tonight. Sometimes when we are not here, you get scared. You wish we would stay with you, but your father and I are going to enjoy a dinner with friends tonight. We'll have dinner at home with you tomorrow." Acknowledge his views *and* stand up for your own.

Acknowledge Your Differences with Optimism

Expressing your agreement with your opponent does not mean suppressing your differences. Indeed, it is often helpful to acknowledge them openly. It assures your opponent that you have understood his side of the story, which helps him relax. In many ethnic conflicts, for example, the parties only feel comfortable acknowledging areas of agreement *after* they have clearly delineated the areas of disagreement.

When you set out your differences, you may find they are not as great as either of you imagined. Sometimes, however, they seem overwhelming. So an optimistic stance on your part is critical. Affirm your interest in reaching agreement and assert your belief that a satisfactory solution is possible: "I think we *can* make a deal here." Be bold in acknowledging your opponent's views, bold in asserting your own, and equally bold in expressing optimism that your differences can be resolved.

Create a Favorable Climate for Negotiation

In sum, the hurdles you face are your opponent's suspicion and hostility, his closed ears, and his lack of respect. Your best strategy is to step to his side. It is harder to be hostile toward someone who hears you out and acknowledges what you say and how you feel. It is easier to listen to someone who has listened to you. And respect breeds respect.

Pleasantly surprised by your behavior, your opponent may think: "This person actually seems to understand and appreciate my problem. Since almost no one else does, that means he must be intelligent." Then comes the clincher: "Maybe I can negotiate with this person after all." That is the crack in the wall you have been seeking.

To conclude, let's return to the negotiation between AT&T and Boeing described at the beginning of the chapter. Faced with the breakdown of the talks, the AT&T sales chief arranged a private meeting with the Boeing purchasing director. This is how he started off:

"I've been trying to understand your concerns. Correct me if I'm mistaken, but as you and your colleagues at Boeing see it, we've been misleading you, saying we're prepared to give all this service but not to put it in writing and be held liable for it. That seems to be bad-faith negotiating. So naturally you get angry and don't see the point in continuing. Is that right?"

"That's right!" the Boeing buyer replied with fervor. "How can we trust what you say? If *we* were negotiating an aircraft sale and told the buyer the safety specifications but then said we wouldn't put them in writing, the buyer would walk right out the door. And he'd be right to leave. If we won't be held accountable, we shouldn't be in the airplane building business. If *you* won't be bound by your promises, you shouldn't be in the communications business!"

"You're absolutely right," acknowledged the AT&T sales chief. *"I'd feel the same way if I were you!"*

Surprised, the Boeing negotiator asked, "Then *why* won't you agree to put your promises in writing and agree to pay damages if you don't live up to your commitment?"

The AT&T representative answered, "We will of course put our promises in writing. Damages are an issue we have trouble with but are at least willing to discuss. First I want to see if I can clear up what's gotten us stuck. I think I'm only beginning to understand it myself. I hear you saying that Boeing has what you might call an 'engineering culture.' There's no tolerance for ambiguity or error when people's lives are at stake. So if you promise a certain safety specification, you'd better be sure you're on target. And, of course, everything has to be clearly specified in writing. Am I making sense?"

"Yes, what you're saying is right, but I don't see what it has to do with our problem," said the Boeing buyer.

"If you'll bear with me, I'll try to explain why I think it has everything to do with our problem. You see, at AT&T we also have our engineers, but we're primarily in the business of providing a service. We're more of a 'relationship culture.' We see our relationship with our clients as all-important—if the client's not happy, we're not happy. That's why people call us 'Ma Bell.' Now, when your mom tells you she's going to make your lunch and drive you to school, you don't say to her, 'Now, Mom, put it in writing and I'm going to hold you liable for damages,' do you?"

"Of course not."

"You just expect that she'll do the best she can. Now obviously there's a big difference between a household and a business, but this gives you a sense of where we're coming from. We make oral promises and fully expect to deliver on them. Our track record, you'll have to admit, is very good. It's a new experience for us to meet with a lot of skepticism and a demand for damages from a client. That's why we sort of collided with each other at the last meeting—you were coming from one place, which was absolutely right for you, and we were coming from another. Does this make any sense to you?"

"It's beginning to. Let me ask you . . ."

And so the negotiations got back under way.

How was the AT&T sales chief able to get the negotiation back on track? He preemptively acknowledged what he understood to be Boeing's concerns. He listened. He didn't try to refute his client's argument or defend AT&T. He simply acknowledged that the client was right. Once the Boeing negotiator's views were understood and appreciated, his anger subsided and he became more receptive. He asked a question, inviting the AT&T representative to offer his explanation. Only then did the sales chief describe how the situation looked from his side. In the end, he was able to allay his client's suspicions, get him to listen, and garner his respect—in short, to disarm him. Not long afterward, AT&T and Boeing reached agreement on the $150 million sale.

STEP THREE

Change the Game

DON'T REJECT . . . REFRAME

Craft against vice I will apply.
—WILLIAM SHAKESPEARE,
Measure for Measure

Now that you have created a favorable climate for negotiation, the next challenge is to change the game. The problem is that while you would like to discuss each side's *interests* and how to satisfy them, your opponent is likely to insist on his *position*. Consider the following negotiation:

BUDGET DIRECTOR: I won't accept anything less than a ten percent cut in your budget. So let's get to it, okay?

MARKETING CHIEF: That's impossible. We can't survive on that.

BUDGET DIRECTOR: I'm sorry, but I've already told the other department heads you'll take the cut. If you don't, all the other deals will unravel.

MARKETING CHIEF: I understand your problem but try to understand mine. I've just instituted a new plan in my department that will bring about greater productivity and substantial cost savings—but I can't implement it with a ten percent cut. Can't we cooperate and try to arrive at a solution that's good for the company?

BUDGET DIRECTOR: That's what I want—your cooperation. Let me put you down for that cut. Deal?

MARKETING CHIEF: I'm sorry, but I just can't agree to that.

BUDGET DIRECTOR: Look, I don't want to get you into any trouble. But I need that budget cut now.

MARKETING CHIEF: Suppose we take a six percent cut. That goes a long way toward meeting your target. How about that?

BUDGET DIRECTOR: Well, that makes it easier. Now you've only got to find four percent more.

MARKETING CHIEF: Six percent is as high as I can go.

BUDGET DIRECTOR: The president is going to hear about this!

What can you do if your opponent takes an inflexible position? What if he digs in ("I won't accept anything less than ten percent"), threatens ("I don't want to get you into any trouble"), or presents you with a *fait accompli* ("I've already told the other department heads that you'll take the cut")?

Since your opponent's demand seems unreasonable, your natural temptation is to reject it out of hand. You respond to his position by advancing your own. He, of course, rejects your position and reasserts his. Even if you come back with a reasonable compromise, he may interpret it as your fallback position, pocket the concession, and press you for more. Before you know it, you are once again playing his game of hardball—precisely what you wanted to avoid.

Is there any way to draw your opponent into *your* game of problem-solving negotiation?

To Change the Game, Change the Frame

To change the game, you need to do the opposite of what you're tempted to do. Instead of rejecting what your opponent says, accept it—and transform it into the negotiation you want to have. In other words, reframe.

Reframing means recasting what your opponent says in a

form that directs attention back to the problem of satisfying both sides' interests. Reframing literally means changing the frame around the picture. In this case, it means putting a problem-solving frame around your opponent's positional statements. You act *as if* he were trying to solve the problem, and thus you draw him into the new game.

Consider this example: In 1979, the SALT II arms control treaty was up for ratification in the U.S. Senate. To obtain the necessary two thirds majority, the Senate leaders wanted to add an amendment, but this required Soviet assent. A young U.S. senator, Joseph R. Biden, Jr., was about to travel to Moscow, so the Senate leadership asked him to raise the question with Soviet Foreign Minister Andrei Gromyko.

The match in Moscow was uneven: a junior senator head to head with a hard-nosed diplomat of vast experience. Gromyko began the discussion with an eloquent hour-long disquisition on how the Soviets had always played catch-up to the Americans in the arms race. He concluded with a forceful argument for why SALT II actually favored the Americans and why, therefore, the Senate should ratify the treaty unchanged. Gromyko's position on the proposed amendment was an unequivocal *nyet.*

Then it was Biden's turn. Instead of arguing with Gromyko and taking a counterposition, he slowly and gravely said, "Mr. Gromyko, you make a very persuasive case. I agree with much of what you've said. When I go back to my colleagues in the Senate, however, and report what you've just told me, some of them—like Senator Goldwater or Senator Helms—will not be persuaded, and I'm afraid their concerns will carry weight with others." Biden went on to explain their worries. "You have more experience in these arms-control matters than anyone else alive. How would *you* advise me to respond to my colleagues' concerns?"

Gromyko could not resist the temptation to offer advice

to the inexperienced young American. He started coaching him on what he should tell the skeptical senators. One by one, Biden raised the arguments that would need to be dealt with, and Gromyko grappled with each of them. In the end, appreciating perhaps for the first time how the amendment would help win wavering votes, Gromyko reversed himself and gave his consent.

Instead of *rejecting* Gromyko's position, which would have led to an argument over positions, Biden acted as if Gromyko were interested in problem-solving and asked for his advice. He *reframed* the conversation as a constructive discussion about how to meet the senators' concerns and win ratification of the treaty.

Reframing works because every message is subject to interpretation. You have the *power of positive perception*, the ability to put a problem-solving frame around whatever your opponent says. He will often go along with your reinterpretation, just as Gromyko did, partly because he is surprised that you have not rejected his position and partly because he is eager to pursue his argument.

Because your opponent is concentrating on the *outcome* of the negotiation, he may not even be aware that you have subtly changed the *process.* Instead of focusing on competing positions, you are figuring out how best to satisfy each side's interests. You don't need to ask your opponent's permission. Just start to play the new game.

Reframing is one of the greatest powers you have as a negotiator. *The way to change the game is to change the frame.*

Ask Problem-Solving Questions

The most obvious way to direct your opponent's attention toward the problem is to tell him about it. But making assertions can easily arouse his resistance. The better approach is to ask questions. Instead of giving your opponent the right answer, try to ask the right question. Instead of trying to teach him yourself, *let the problem be his teacher.*

The single most valuable tool in reframing is the problem-solving question. A problem-solving question focuses attention on the interests of each side, the options for satisfying them, and the standards of fairness for resolving differences. Here are some of the most useful questions:

Ask Why

Instead of treating your opponent's position as an obstacle, treat it as an opportunity. When he tells you his position, he is giving you valuable information about what he wants. Invite him to tell you more by asking, "Why is it that you want that?," "What is the problem?," or "What are your concerns?" Find out what really motivates him. As he answers, note what happens. The focus of conversation shifts from his position to his interests. You are suddenly engaged in problem-solving negotiation.

How you ask something is just as important as *what* you ask. If direct questions sound confrontational, put them in an indirect form: "I'm not sure I understand why you want that," "Help me to see why this is important to you," or "You seem to feel pretty strongly about this—I'd be interested in understanding why." It helps to preface your question with an acknowledgment: "I hear what you're saying. I'm sure the company policy has a good purpose—could you please explain it to me?" In showing your interest and respect, remember that your tone, facial expressions, and body language are just as important as your words.

Asking questions to uncover interests is like peeling the

layers of an onion. You uncover one layer after another, as in the following conversation:

"Why do you want to leave the job?" asked the senior partner in a New York law firm.

"Because I need more money and you can't give me enough of a raise," replied the young associate.

"What's the problem?"

"Well, my wife and I just had another child, and we need to move into a larger apartment."

"So what's the problem?"

"We can't find one that's rent-controlled."

Once the senior partner had gotten to the bottom of the problem, he used his network to find the associate an apartment that fit the bill. The associate ended up staying with the firm for thirty more years, becoming a senior partner himself. Persistent probing of underlying interests helped produce a mutually satisfying agreement.

Remember that the relevant interests are not only your opponent's but his constituents' as well. His hard-line position may have less to do with his concerns than with those of his boss, board of directors, stockholders, union members, or family. Ask about *their* interests too.

Ask Why Not

If your opponent is reluctant to reveal his interests, take an indirect tack. If asking *why* doesn't work, try asking *why not.* Propose an option and ask "Why not do it this way?" or "What would be wrong with this approach?" People reluctant to disclose their concerns usually love to criticize. If you are immersed in a budget negotiation and ask "Why shouldn't we cut the budget for marketing?" the marketing chief may well answer, "I'll tell you why. Sales will plunge, the board will start breathing down our necks, and I'll end up typing up a new résumé." Without being aware of it, he has just given you valuable information about his interests —his concerns about sales, his worries about pressure from the board, and his fear of losing his job.

If your counterpart still won't reveal his interests, bring them up yourself and ask him to correct you. If you are trying to persuade a reluctant manufacturer to speed up production, you could say to him, "If I understand what you're saying, your interests are in keeping costs down, quality high, and the service reliable. Is that right?" Few people can resist the temptation to correct someone's misunderstanding of their interests. The manufacturer may reply, "That's not exactly right. You've forgotten about . . ." and off he goes telling you about his interests.

If your opponent still resists, it may be because he fears you will use the information to take advantage of him. To build trust and set him at ease, tell him your interests first: "I'd like to speed up production in order to take advantage of the new market. My distributors are breathing down my neck for the product, and personally, I feel my credibility is on the line. Can you tell me a little about the constraints that make it hard for you to speed up production?" If revealing your interests makes you feel vulnerable, you don't need to tell all at the start. Give your opponent a little information about your interests, ask him about his, then give him more information, and so on. Build trust incrementally.

Ask What If

The next step is to engage your opponent in discussing options. To introduce a host of possible solutions *without* challenging your opponent's position, use one of the most powerful phrases in the English language: "What if?"

Suppose your customer announces, "That's all the money we have in the budget to pay for this consulting project. We can't pay a penny more!" Ask him, "*What if* we were to stretch out the project so that the excess could go into next year's budget?" Or, "*What if* we were to reduce the magnitude of the project to fit within your budget constraints?" Or, "*What if* we can help you show your boss how the benefits to your company justify asking for a budget increase?" If you can get him to address any one of these questions, you will have succeeded in changing the game. Suddenly he is exploring options with you.

Turn the conversation into a brainstorming session. Take your counterpart's position and reframe it as one possible option among many. Suppose, for instance, you are having a difficult family negotiation about where to spend the Christmas holidays. Your spouse insists on going to his or her family's home. Instead of rejecting the proposal, you could say, "That's one possibility." Propose an option or two yourself and invite your spouse to suggest others: "Another possibility, of course, would be to spend it with my family. Or what if we divide it between the two—Christmas with yours and New Year's with mine? Got any other ideas?"

If your counterpart begins to criticize your options, you might say "I'd like to hear your criticism, but can we put it off until we have all the options on the table? Then we can see which works best." Since judging inhibits creativity, invent first and evaluate later.

Ask for Your Opponent's Advice

Another way to engage your opponent in a discussion of options is to ask for his advice. It is probably the last thing he expects you to do. Ask "What would you suggest that I do?" "What would you do if you were in my shoes?" Or "What would you say to my constituents?" This is the approach Senator Biden took with Minister Gromyko.

It is flattering to be asked for advice. You are, in effect, acknowledging your opponent's competence and status. It not only disarms him, but it also gives you a chance to educate him about your problem and the constraints facing you.

Imagine you have to get approval for an exception to company policy from a bureaucrat known for his rigidity. You anticipate that if you ask him directly, he will complain loudly about you and all the others who are trying to bend the rules. So instead you say, "Mr. Talbot, you have been recommended to me as an expert on company policy. I have a problem on which I would like to seek your advice." After explaining the situation, you ask, "How would you suggest that I proceed?"

Once your counterpart gets involved in your problem, he begins to develop a stake in living up to the positive and powerful role in which you have cast him. Often he will come up with a solution to your problem; Mr. Talbot may grant an exception to the policy.

If, however, he responds by reasserting the policy, acknowledge his concerns and continue to ask for his advice: "I recognize the reasons for this policy. It's important that you uphold it. Still, this project is very important for the company's future. How would you suggest we get it accomplished?" If Mr. Talbot says there is nothing *he* can do, then say, "I understand. Could you advise me about who could grant an exception?"

Asking for advice is one of the most effective ways you can change the game.

Ask "What Makes That Fair?"

Your opponent's position may strike you as unreasonable. Instead of rejecting it, however, you can use it as a jumping-off point for a discussion of standards of fairness. Act as if he must believe his position is fair—he usually does. Tell him: "You must have good reasons for thinking that's a fair solution. I'd like to hear them."

Suppose, for example, an important client informs you that he expects free service to be thrown in with the price of the product. You may feel you can't say no without offending the client. Yet if you say yes, it will be an expensive decision. So you ask him: "What's your thinking about what makes that fair? Does our competition throw in the service for free?" You are using a standard of fairness—in this case, market practice—so that he can see for himself that his demand is unfair. As the French philosopher Blaise Pascal wrote more than three centuries ago: "People are usually more convinced by reasons they discovered by themselves than by those found by others."

In one acquisitions negotiation, the seller asked what seemed an excessively high price for the company. Instead of rejecting the price, the buyer set out to educate him. He began by asking what profits the seller expected his company to make in the first year. The seller answered, "We will do four million this year, and that equals four hundred thousand in profits." Once the buyer had this optimistic point of reference, he was able to say, "I'm sure you'll meet that goal if you say you will. After all, you're running a hell of a ship here. But the price of that ship is based on your estimate. You know better than I the number of things that can throw that off. If you don't meet that projection, do we get a reduction in price?" By probing for the rationale behind the price, the buyer was able to win a considerable reduction without ever rejecting the price flat out.

Sometimes, to start a discussion about a fair outcome, you may need to propose a standard yourself. In the acquisitions negotiation the buyer suggested using standard accounting practice to determine a fair price. He told the seller: "My accountant has brought up a point, though I'm sure it's something you're already aware of. We're probably going to have to set up a receivables reserve of about half a million dollars. . . . It's a sound accounting practice, considering the way your company looks. This could bring down the company's net worth and will mean we have to take a much harder look at the price tag you've put on it." The seller again lowered his price substantially.

If your opponent rejects your standard, challenge him to come up with a better one. A discussion of different standards will still achieve your objective of shifting the focus from positions to fair outcomes.

Make Your Questions Open-Ended

Not any question will do. A problem-solving question needs to be open-ended and eye-opening.

How you phrase the question determines the answer. When a company or government official says, "You can't do that; it's against our policy," you may be tempted to ask, "Can't the policy be changed?" And the answer you will undoubtedly receive is a resounding no. If you had thought about it beforehand, you might have anticipated the answer. In effect, your question set you up for a no.

Your opponent can easily answer no to questions prefaced by "is," "isn't," "can," or "can't." So ask a question that cannot be answered by no. In other words, make it open-ended. Preface your question with "how," "why,"

"why not," "what," or "who." Your opponent cannot easily answer no to questions such as "What's the purpose of this policy?" "Who has the authority to grant an exception?" and "How would you advise me to proceed?"

Too often people ask questions for which their opponent has a ready-made response. Consider the example of a British arms-control negotiator who, no matter what he proposed to his Soviet counterpart, always received the same monosyllabic answer: *"Nyet."* After a year of this treatment, the Briton took the Soviet aside and expressed his exasperation. The Soviet negotiator replied, "It is *just* as frustrating for me to negotiate with such inflexible instructions from Moscow. The problem is that you're always asking me questions for which I have instructions. Why don't you ask me questions for which I have *no* instructions?" Puzzled, the British diplomat nevertheless complied at their next negotiating session, posing a new, eye-opening question. The Soviet negotiator thanked him politely and told him that since he had no instructions on how to answer, he would have to return to Moscow. There, he was able to persuade his Kremlin superiors to give him the flexibility needed to reach agreement.

Taking a cue from the two diplomats, you need to ask questions for which your opponent has no "instructions," no pat answer. Your questions should make him think—just as Biden's queries compelled Gromyko to contend with the senators' reservations. In considering your questions, your opponent may change his mind and become more amenable to agreement.

Tap the Power of Silence

Only half the power of a problem-solving question lies in the question itself. The other half can be found in the pregnant silence that follows as your opponent struggles with the question and mulls over his answer. A common mistake is to deprive him of this creative time. If he does not respond, you may feel a growing discomfort from the silence. In normal conversation, when you see that your question has made the other person uncomfortable, you let him off the hook by breaking the silence.

You should resist this temptation and wait for an answer from your opponent. After all, you have asked a perfectly legitimate question. Let the silence and discomfort work on his mind. He may eventually respond with information about his interests, or a possible option, or a relevant standard. The moment he does he is engaged in the game of problem-solving negotiation.

Remember, it takes only one answer to get you going. So be persistent. If one question doesn't yield the results you are seeking, try another angle, just as a skillful interviewer would. If you observe the practice of successful negotiators, you will find that they ask countless questions.

Reframe Tactics

Problem-solving questions enable you to reframe your opponent's *position* in terms of interests, options, and standards. But you also need to deal with his *tactics*, the stone walls, attacks, and tricks he uses to get you to give in to his position. How do you reframe his tactics so as to direct his attention toward the problem?

Go Around Stone Walls

What if your opponent locks himself into an extreme position, tells you "take it or leave it," or sets a rigid deadline?

To go around a stone wall, you can ignore it, reinterpret it, or test it.

Ignore the stone wall. If your opponent declares "Take it or leave it!" or "You have until five o'clock or the deal is off!" you cannot be sure whether he means it or is just bluffing. So test his seriousness by ignoring the tactic. Keep talking about the problem as if you didn't hear what he said, or change the subject altogether. If he is serious, he will repeat his message.

Reinterpret the stone wall as an aspiration. Suppose a union leader announces to you: "I've told my people that if I don't come back with a fifteen percent raise, they can have my head on a silver platter." He has locked himself in. If you challenge his commitment, you will only make it harder for him to back away. Instead, reinterpret his commitment as an aspiration and direct attention back to the problem: "We all have our aspirations, I guess. Management is under pressure from the downturn in the economy and would love to cut wages. But I think we'll both be better off being realistic and taking a hard look at the merits of the pay issue. What are other companies paying their workers for the same job?" Your reinterpretation makes it easier for him to make a graceful exit from his commitment.

Or imagine you have to deal with a rigid deadline laid down by your opponent. Instead of rejecting it, you can soften it by reinterpreting it as a target: "We would all like to conclude this negotiation by then. That would be ideal. We'd better get to work immediately." Then turn to the problem with great gusto to show your good will.

Take the stone wall seriously, but test it. A third approach is to test the stone wall to see if it's real. For instance, treat your opponent's deadline seriously, but as it approaches, arrange to be called away for an urgent phone call or meeting. Hostage negotiators, for example, will find some credible but "uncontrollable" event, such as a bank holiday, that makes it impossible for them to assemble the ransom money in time to meet the terrorists' deadline. One leading negotiator explains, "We like deadlines. The shorter, the better. Because once you've broken the deadline, you've knocked them off their game plan."

Another way to test a stone wall without directly challenging it is to ask questions. If a car salesman declares that the price is final, you can ask whether you could get financing or a good trade for your old car. If the salesman begins to show flexibility, you will have determined that the price may not in fact be final.

Don't forget that you can sometimes turn your opponent's stone wall to your advantage. If he has given you an inflexible deadline, for example, you can say, "I'd like to be able to convene the board to make you a more generous offer, but *in view of the time problem,* this is the best I can do at the moment." Or "To meet *your* deadline, we'll need your help. Can you take care of pick-up and delivery?"

Deflect Attacks

What if your opponent threatens you, insults you, or blames you for something that has gone wrong? How can you reframe an attack, shifting the focus away from you toward the problem?

Ignore the attack. One approach is to pretend you didn't hear the attack and go on talking about the problem. Suppose you're a union leader dealing with a difficult boss who threatens to fire half the work force unless you give in to his demands for wage cuts. Drawing attention to the threat would just make it harder for him to back away. Replying "Don't be ridiculous. You'd never do it!" may only spur him on to prove he meant what he said. Instead, you should ignore the threat and focus on the company's financial plight: "I know you're under pressure to make your numbers look better. Tell me a little about our situation."

If your opponent sees that his abusive tactics do not work, he will often stop. Take the buyer who liked to keep his vendors waiting outside his office in order to unsettle them and make them more pliable on the terms of the deal. One vendor decided to ignore the tactic, bringing a novel along to read. When the buyer finally ushered him in, the vendor made a show of reluctantly closing the book, as if he had not been inconvenienced in the slightest. When the buyer took a long phone call in the middle of the meeting, out came the novel. After two or three such meetings, the buyer realized the tactic wasn't working and stopped using it.

Reframe an attack on you as an attack on the problem. A second approach is to reinterpret the attack. Suppose you are trying to win departmental approval for a new product, and a co-worker takes you to task: "Don't you know any better than to submit a proposal that will never fly?" You could become defensive and hostile. *Or* you could ignore the personal criticism, acknowledge the point, and reinterpret it as an attack on the problem: "You may have a point there. How would you improve the proposal to make it fly?"

Your attacker is making two claims: first, that your proposal is no good; and second, that *you* are no good. You have the power to choose which claim you want to address. By choosing the more legitimate concern about the proposal, you can effectively sidestep the personal attack and direct your opponent's attention toward the problem.

Reframe a personal attack as friendly. Another way of reframing a personal attack is to misinterpret it as friendly. Take the eighteenth-century general who had fallen into disfavor with the great Prussian warrior king, Frederick the Great. Coming upon the king, the general saluted him with the greatest respect, but Frederick turned his back. "I am happy to see that Your Majesty is no longer angry with me," murmured the general. "How so?" demanded Frederick. "Because Your Majesty has never in his life turned his back on an enemy," replied the general. Disarmed, Frederick took the general back into his favor.

In everyday life you can reframe a personal attack as a show of concern and shift the focus back to the problem. For example, if your opponent tries to unsettle you by saying "You know you don't look too good. You sure you feel all right?" you could answer, "Thanks for your concern. I feel great now that we're getting close to agreement."

Reframe from past wrongs to future remedies. Your opponent's attack often takes the form of blame. In a discussion of the household budget, a husband accuses his wife: "You waste money on useless knickknacks! Remember that seventy-five-dollar ceramic cat you bought?" The wife retorts, "Well, what about you, Mr. Showboat, taking all your pals out for drinks last week? How much did *that* cost?" And on they go for hours, sniping about the past. The budget is forgotten.

The opportunity always exists to reframe the issue from the past to the future, from who was wrong to what can be done about the problem. The wife can say to her husband:

"Yes, Ben, we both agreed it was too much to pay for the ceramic cat. I won't make the same mistake again. Now what about next month's budget? How do we make sure we keep to it?" When your opponent criticizes you for a past incident, don't miss the opportunity to ask "How do we make sure it never happens again?" Reframe the blame as joint responsibility for tackling the problem.

Reframe from "you" and "me" to "we." When husband and wife are quarreling about their budget, all you hear is *"You* did this!" and *"I* did not!" A simple change in language from "you" and "me" to "we" can help. The wife asks, "How do *we* make sure *we* stay within the budget?" "We" creates a side-by-side stance, drawing attention to common interests and shared goals.

A simple and powerful way to reframe the situation from "you" or "me" to "we" is through body language. When people argue, they usually stand or sit face to face, physically expressing their confrontation. So find a natural excuse to sit side by side. Pull out a document or proposed agreement and sit down next to your counterpart to review it. Or sit next to your spouse on the sofa instead of shouting across the kitchen counter. Talking side by side will not magically transform the situation, but it will reinforce the idea that you are partners facing a tough challenge together.

Expose Tricks

The toughest tactic to reframe is a trick. Tricks take advantage of common assumptions made in good-faith negotiation—that the other person is telling the truth, that he will deliver on his promises, that he does have the authority he implies he has, and that once an issue is resolved, it won't be renegotiated. Tricks are hard to reframe because they are already couched in the language of cooperation and reasonableness in order to deceive you.

You could, of course, challenge the trick directly, but the risks are high. For one thing, you might be mistaken. And even if you are right, your opponent is likely to take offense at being called a cheat or liar, and your relationship will suffer.

The alternative to rejecting the trick is to play along with it. Respond *as if* your opponent were negotiating in good faith, but act a little slow and ask probing questions in order to test his sincerity. In other words, *play dumb like a fox.* If your opponent is sincere, your questions will do no harm. If he is trying to deceive you, you will expose the trick. Since you have not confronted him, he can save face by pretending it was all a mistake or a misunderstanding.

Ask clarifying questions. Ask questions to check and clarify your opponent's assertions. If you are purchasing a company and the seller has included outstanding accounts receivable in the company's net worth, say in a nonjudgmental tone, "You must have good reasons for believing that these accounts receivable will in fact be paid. I'd be interested in knowing why you think so." Check his assumptions when he quotes "infallible" authorities or methodologies such as computers and spreadsheets. Don't hesitate to press a little. And watch for ambiguities in his answers as well as outright evasions. If you spot a contradiction, don't challenge it directly. Just act confused: "I'm sorry, I'm afraid I don't understand. Could you explain how this relates to what you said before?"

One way to test your suspicions is to ask your opponent questions to which you already know the answers. You can learn a lot from observing how he shades his responses.

A common trick is to mislead you into believing that he has decision-making authority when he doesn't. You may use up all your flexibility only to discover that he has to get the approval of his boss or board, who may well ask for additional concessions. To protect yourself, ask questions early on to clarify your opponent's authority: "Am I correct in assuming you have the authority to settle this matter?" Make sure you get a specific answer. If he doesn't have full authority, find out who else must agree and how long it will take to get the answer.

Another common trick is the last-minute demand *after* you have reached agreement. Instead of challenging the demand, you can ask, "Are you suggesting that we reopen the negotiation?" If he says no, you can say, "Well then, I think we should just stick with the agreement we've already reached." If, however, he says yes, you can say, "All right. We'll treat it as a joint draft to which neither side is committed. You check with your boss, and I'll check with mine, and let's meet tomorrow to discuss possible changes." If he wants something extra, you should get something in return.

Make a reasonable request. You have one advantage in dealing with a trickster that you don't have with someone who is openly uncooperative, and that is his stake in appearing reasonable. So take him at his word and put it to the test, thereby placing him in a dilemma. Either he lives up to his pretense of cooperation or he drops the sham altogether. In other words, you can administer a "reasonable request test."

Design a reasonable request that your opponent would agree to if he was genuinely cooperative. If, for instance, you suspect he might be concealing debts that are difficult to collect, say "If you don't mind, I'd like to have my accountant look over your books and check the accounts receivable, just as a standard business routine." If the seller refuses to let your accountant go over his books, he will look uncooperative, and you can conclude that you can't rely on what he has told you.

If your opponent cites a "hard-hearted partner" as justification for an additional demand, you can make the following request: "Excuse me, Jerry. I'm not sure I understand. Did we make a mistake in not including your bankers in our previous discussions? I hate to think that I've put you on the spot here. Maybe I should get together with them and go over the terms we discussed. Can you arrange a meeting?"

Jerry now has a choice. He can let you meet with the bankers—which should give you a better sense of their objections and whether this is indeed a trick. Or he can refuse to let you meet with them—which should put you on your guard. Or he can drop the tactic altogether and stick to the original agreement. Whatever the outcome, you are free to follow up with further reasonable requests and clarifying questions.

Turn the trick to your advantage. If you see through your opponent's trick, you can often turn it to your advantage. Suppose you are representing the wife in a divorce case. The husband promises to pay child support, but you have reason to believe he will fail to do so. When you raise your concern, his lawyer protests that his client will certainly pay.

"Are you certain?" you ask.

"Absolutely, my client is an honorable man," replies his lawyer.

"Then he will surely not object to adding a clause that in the case of three months' nonpayment, my client will receive his equity in the house in substitution for child support."

The more vigorously the lawyer has affirmed his client's reliability, the harder it will be to object.

Negotiate About the Rules of the Game

If, despite all your efforts, your opponent continues to resort to stone walls, attacks, and tricks, you need to reframe the conversation in yet another way. Recast it as a negotiation *about* the negotiation.

There are actually two "negotiations" going on. One is the negotiation about *substance:* the terms and conditions, dollars and cents. The second is the negotiation about the *rules of the game.* How is the negotiation to be conducted? If you watch parents and children, for instance, negotiating over everyday issues such as bedtime, you will observe that they are also constantly renegotiating the extent to which temper tantrums, threats, and bribes are acceptable tactics.

Usually this second negotiation remains tacit. If you haven't been successful in changing the game, however, you need to make this negotiation explicit. You need to talk about your opponent's behavior. Often it is sufficient simply to bring it up.

Bring It Up

The person who uses tactics is usually probing to see exactly what he can get away with. In order to get him to stop, you may need to *let him know you know* what he is doing. Bringing up his tactic sends the message "I wasn't born yesterday. I know the game you're playing. Your tactic isn't going to work." If your opponent wants an agreement, he will drop the tactic, because using it will only make agreement more difficult to reach.

The problem is that your opponent may mistake your calling attention to his tactic as an attack. The secret is to reframe his tactic as an interesting contribution rather than as an underhanded trick.

Consider an example. Liz and Pam are two young lawyers trying to buy a set of used labor-law books from two established attorneys, Bob and Charlie. At the outset of the discussion, Bob announces in a firm voice, "The very least we'll accept for these books is $13,000. You can take it or leave it." Charlie, however, argues with his partner Bob: "Come on, these two are just starting out. Surely we can give them a break. How about calling it $11,000 and leaving it at that?" A fair market price for the books would be $7,000, but Bob and Charlie have orchestrated a little drama in which Bob plays the bad guy who sets out an extreme demand, and Charlie plays the good guy who, by contrast, appears reasonable. In many instances the extreme demand might have its intended effect of pressuring Liz and Pam into accepting Charlie's offer for fear that Bob might change Charlie's mind.

In this instance, however, Liz responds by saying, "That's interesting. . . ." She pauses for a second, giving herself a chance to think. Then she suddenly bursts out laughing and exclaims admiringly, "You guys are terrific! That is the *best* good-guy bad-guy routine I've seen in years. Did you plan it, or was it just a coincidence? Seriously now, let's see if we can establish a *fair* price for the books."

Bob and Charlie don't quite know how to respond. They can't really be offended, since Liz is complimenting them and they aren't sure whether she is serious. In any case, to pursue the tactic would be pointless. It works only when the other person is not aware of it. Having neutralized the tactic without alienating their opponents, Liz and Pam can proceed to discuss the purchase on its merits.

It is important that you bring up the tactic without appearing to attack your opponent personally. Calling him a liar or a cheat does not make him more receptive to problem-solving negotiation. By showing admiration for Charlie and Bob's skill and making light of the tactic, Liz helps them save face. Her interest is not in scoring points, but in purchasing a set of law books for a fair price and in fostering a working relationship with an established law firm.

You should make it easy for your opponent to drop his tactic. If he is being particularly rude, for instance, point it out by offering him an explanation or an excuse: "It sounds like you're having a rough day." If he threatens you, respond as one businesswoman did. Instead of challenging her opponent by saying "Don't threaten me," she asked in a calm and somewhat surprised tone, "You're not intending to threaten me, are you?" Her question of clarification offered her opponent a graceful way out. He took it, saying, "Who me? No, I'm not threatening you." In case you have misinterpreted the other side's behavior, such an approach ensures that little if any harm will come of it.

Don't accuse your opponent. Just make note of what he is doing. If he constantly interrupts you, look him in the eye, use his name, and say "Mike, you interrupted me." Or ask "May I finish my sentence?" Use a nonconfrontational, matter-of-fact tone. If he does it again, patiently remind him, perhaps with a little gentle prodding. "Hey, you're interrupting me." Think of yourself as a friend giving him some useful feedback. Call him on his behavior—nicely.

Negotiate about the Negotiation

If bringing it up isn't sufficient, then you may need to have a full-fledged negotiation about the rules of the game.

Take your opponent aside and tell him: "It seems to me the way we're negotiating isn't going to lead to the kind of outcome we both want. We need to stop arguing about the issues and discuss the rules of the game." More informally, you could say "Something's bothering me, and I'd like to talk it over with you."

Negotiate about the process just as you would about the

substance. Identify *interests,* generate *options* for how best to negotiate, and discuss *standards* of fair behavior. If, for example, he refuses to talk about anything except his position, you might tell him: "My interest is in achieving a mutually satisfactory agreement efficiently and amicably. As I see it, in order for us to accomplish this we have to be willing to listen to each other, share information about our interests, and brainstorm together. We ought to be able to expand the pie, not just divide it up. If I understand your interests better, I can help you meet them, and you can do the same for me. Shall we give it a try?"

Without questioning your opponent's honesty, discuss the fairness of particular tactics: "What if *I* were to ask for additional concessions *after* we reached agreement? Would you consider that a legitimate tactic?"

Make a specific request for how you would like your opponent to change his behavior. If your opponent continues to attack you personally, you can say calmly, "I'm willing to talk about this whenever you are willing to stop attacking me." If you are a CEO approached by a corporate raider seeking information about your company, you could tell him: "Look, if you're willing to rule out a hostile takeover, I'll be happy to talk candidly. Otherwise, I'll have to assume that you'll use the information I give you against me."

Once you have agreed on the rules, you can return to negotiating over the substance in a more constructive and productive manner.

The Turning Point

The turning point of the breakthrough method is when you change the game from positional bargaining to problem-solving negotiation. The key to changing the game is to reframe. Reframing means taking whatever your opponent says and directing it against the problem. Remember the batting secret of the great home-run hitter Sadaharu Oh, the Japanese Babe Ruth. Oh said that he looked on the opposing pitcher as his *partner,* who with every pitch was serving up an *opportunity* for him to hit a home run. Similarly, you should see your opponent as a partner who, with his every position and tactic, is offering you an opportunity to talk about the problem.

Consider how, in the example at the beginning of this chapter, the marketing chief might have used reframing to draw the budget director into a new game:

BUDGET DIRECTOR *(digging in to his position):* I won't accept anything less than a ten percent cut in your budget. So let's get to it, okay?

MARKETING CHIEF *(asking a problem-solving question):* I recognize the need to cut the company budget, and my department is prepared to contribute its share. Just help me understand why you need that much.

BUDGET DIRECTOR *(presenting a* fait accompli *and making a threat):* The only way we can get the required savings is if each department takes a ten percent cut. I've already told the other department heads that you'll take the cut. If you don't, all the other deals will unravel, and the president will hear about it.

MARKETING CHIEF *(ignoring the threat and reinterpreting the* fait accompli *as a problem to be solved):* I understand what you're saying. If I were to cut any less, you'd have a big problem explaining that to all the other departments, right?

BUDGET DIRECTOR *(applying pressure):* That's right. So let me put you down for that cut. Deal?

MARKETING CHIEF *(ignoring the pressure and reframing the problem as a joint opportunity):* You know, we've got a real opportunity to save more than the ten percent. It would really help the company and make both of us look very good.

BUDGET DIRECTOR: Oh, what's that?

MARKETING CHIEF *(asking for advice):* As you know, my department has just instituted a new plan that will bring about greater productivity and substantial cost savings. But there are start-up costs we've calculated at five percent of our budget. You have more experience in these matters than anyone else. How can we find the funds to implement the plan and still keep your other deals from unraveling?

BUDGET DIRECTOR: I don't know. . . .

MARKETING CHIEF *(asking a problem-solving question):* Could we explain to the other department heads that my department is taking a five percent cut this year in order to bring even greater savings next year?

BUDGET DIRECTOR: I don't think that will work.

MARKETING CHIEF *(asking a "what if" question):* What if I were to commit to a specific figure of just how much we'll save next year?

BUDGET DIRECTOR: That might help. But that still doesn't solve the problem this year of where to make up the extra savings if you take only a partial cut. Look, I see what you're getting at, but what am I going to tell the president? It's not going to fly.

MARKETING CHIEF *(asking another "what if" question):* What if I talked to the president and sold him on the idea?

BUDGET DIRECTOR: Good luck!

MARKETING CHIEF: I know. It may not be easy. But can I have your support?

BUDGET DIRECTOR: Let me see your plan again. I want to check and make sure your numbers aren't pie in the sky.

MARKETING CHIEF: I'll have it to you within the hour. Thanks for giving me this chance.

The marketing chief has not yet won the agreement he is seeking, but he has won the negotiation over the rules of the game. By reframing, he has turned a positional confrontation into a problem-solving negotiation. He and the budget director are now on their way toward negotiating a mutually satisfactory agreement.

STEP FOUR

Make It Easy to Say Yes

BUILD THEM A GOLDEN BRIDGE

Build your adversary a golden bridge to retreat across.
—SUN TZU

Even after you have disarmed your opponent and engaged him in a problem-solving negotiation, you still have to bring him to a concrete agreement. Things can still go wrong—as they all too often do.

A classic example is the failure of what might have been the world's biggest media merger. Every story has two sides; this is Al Neuharth's account of how he, in his own words, "blew the big one." In 1985, CBS was fighting a hostile takeover bid by media mogul Ted Turner. Neuharth, president of Gannett, had long had his eye on CBS and had cultivated a cordial relationship with CBS president Tom Wyman. Neuharth arranged an exploratory meeting with Wyman to discuss the possibility of a merger that would enable CBS to resist the takeover.

After several meetings the two men reached agreement on most of the basic issues. They decided that because of his age and greater experience, Neuharth would become chairman and CEO, while Wyman would become president and chief operating officer. In a draft press release that Neuharth showed Wyman, Neuharth proposed that the new company be called Universal Media.

Then executives from both companies began ironing out the details. This is how Neuharth, in his memoir, describes the collapse of the talks:

A dozen bankers, lawyers and executives were assembled around the long rectangular table. Tom and I sat side by side. I was really pissed that people in this room for nearly three days had been unable or unwilling to do what Wyman and I had agreed upon. . . . I didn't waste a lot of time with social niceties:

"Tom and I thought it might help if the two CEOs got in on the act and explained to all of you how to get this deal done. It's pretty damn simple. . . . Tom and I have agreed on the management structure of the company. The directors will be seven [CBS], seven [Gannett], and one [jointly selected]. I will be chairman and CEO. Tom will be president and chief operating officer."

The CBS guys looked surprised and puzzled. Our people nodded and smiled.

"You don't have to argue about this or even talk about it or think about it. It's all settled."

Wyman looked uncomfortable. He sat up straight in his chair. "Yes, we've agreed on that," he said a bit hesitantly. . . .

I sensed immediately that I had screwed up. I had come on too directly and forcefully. Wyman's people were hearing this news for the first time from me, not from him. . . . I should have let Wyman explain the terms. He could have put a more gentle face on it. I had satisfied my ego at the expense of crushing his.

Two days later Wyman telephoned to call off the deal. He objected to changing CBS's name and was angry because he had learned Neuharth had also been discussing a merger with Time Inc.

After Neuharth hung up the phone he turned to his executives and said, "The game's over. We lose. And he'll lose."

Obstacles to Agreement

After exploring each side's interests and the options for agreement, you may be ready to deal. But when you make your proposal, your opponent may stall. His resistance can take various forms: lack of interest in your proposals, vague statements, delays, reneging on agreements, or a flat no. In the case of the media merger, CBS's resistance manifested itself in the stymied negotiations between the two teams.

We often blame our opponent's resistance on his personality or basic nature, but behind the impasse usually lie some very good reasons. Consider the four most common ones:

Not his idea. Your opponent may reject your proposal simply because "it wasn't invented here." Neuharth failed to involve Wyman in choosing the new name and in presenting the merger terms to the assembled executives.

Unmet interests. You may be overlooking one of your opponent's basic interests. CBS did not relish the thought of giving up its name.

Fear of losing face. No one wants to look bad to his constituents. Neuharth attributed the failure of the CBS-Gannett merger in large part to having made Wyman lose face in front of his own people.

Too much too fast. Your counterpart may resist because the prospect of agreeing appears overwhelming. The decision seems too big and the time too short. It may seem easier just to say no.

Between his position and the proposed agreement your opponent may see a chasm filled with dissatisfaction, uncertainty, and fear. How can you persuade him to cross it?

Build a Golden Bridge

Frustrated by your opponent's resistance, you may be tempted to push—to cajole, to insist, and to apply pressure. Neuharth pushed hard when the negotiations bogged down.

But pushing may actually make it more difficult for your counterpart to agree. It underscores the fact that the proposal is your idea, not his. It fails to address his unmet interests. It makes it harder for him to go along without appearing to be giving in to your pressure. And it makes the prospect of agreement seem, if anything, more overwhelming.

Consequently, your opponent is likely to resist all the more. In fact, he may welcome your pressure, for it takes him off the hook of having to make a difficult decision. By pushing, Neuharth actually widened the chasm that Wyman had to cross in order to reach agreement.

Instead of pushing your opponent toward an agreement, you need to do the opposite. You need to *draw* him in the direction you want him to move. Your job is to *build a golden bridge* across the chasm. You need to reframe a retreat from his position as an advance toward a better solution.

Take the simple example of how, as a teenager, filmmaker Steven Spielberg built a golden bridge for a tormenting bully:

When I was about thirteen, one local bully gave me nothing but grief all year long. He would knock me down on the grass, or hold my head in the drinking fountain, or push my face in the dirt and give me bloody noses when we had to play football in phys. ed. . . . This was somebody I feared. He was my nemesis. . . . Then, I figured, if you can't beat him, try to get him to join you. So I said to him, "I'm trying to make a movie about fighting the Nazis, and I want you to play this war hero." At first, he laughed in my face, but later he said yes. He was this big fourteen-year-old who looked like John Wayne. I made him the squad leader in the film, with helmet, fatigues, and backpack. After that, he became my best friend.

Young Spielberg discovered the secret of building your adversary a golden bridge. He recognized that the bully needed to feel important. By offering the bully an alternative path to recognition, Spielberg successfully negotiated a ceasefire and turned him into a friend.

Building a golden bridge isn't easy. In a tough negotiation, you might ideally bring in a mediator to help resolve your differences. But that may be neither appropriate nor feasible. So, in the absence of a third party, you need to *mediate your own agreement.*

Instead of starting from where you are, which is everyone's natural instinct, you need to *start from where your opponent is* in order to guide him toward an eventual agreement. One of the best descriptions of this process comes from a French novel. In it, a master diplomat explains, "I turn towards the other man; I become familiar with his situation; I mold myself on his destiny and, living in his place, I begin to experience his fortune and misfortune. Henceforth my concern is not so much to impose my point of view on him, as to persuade him to adopt the one I consider best for him —which always agrees with the interests of my own cause."

Building a golden bridge means making it easier for your opponent to surmount the four common obstacles to agreement: It means actively involving him in devising a solution so that it becomes his idea, not just yours; it means satisfying his unmet interests; it means helping him save face; and it means making the process of negotiation as easy as possible.

Involve Your Opponent

One of the most common negotiating mistakes is to announce that *you* have found the solution to the problem. City planners unveil their scheme for a new waste-disposal site without having involved the residents of the surrounding neighborhood; in response, a citizens' group immediately organizes to fight the project. Management announces a streamlined work plan without having consulted its employees; the workers secretly sabotage the plan. The national budget director and the President's chief of staff closet themselves with six congressional leaders and emerge with an agreed-upon set of budget cuts; members of Congress who weren't involved denounce the agreement and reject it in the subsequent vote. So, too, your opponent is likely to reject your proposal if he had no role in shaping it.

Negotiation is not just a technical problem-solving exercise but a political process in which the different parties must participate and craft an agreement *together*. The process is just as important as the product. You may feel frustrated that negotiations take as long as they do, but remember that negotiation is a ritual—a ritual of participation. People see things differently when they become involved. Your opponent may make allowances he would not otherwise make. He may become comfortable with ideas he once rejected. As he infuses *his* ideas into the proposal, he makes it his own.

Ask for and Build on Your Opponent's Ideas

The great temptation in negotiation is to *tell*. Tell your opponent the way to solve the problem. Tell him why your solution is good for him. Neuharth dealt with the sensitive issue of the new company name by telling Wyman in a draft press release that it should be called Universal Media. Not surprisingly, the idea didn't fly.

Negotiation is more about asking than it is about telling. The simplest way to involve your opponent is to ask him for his ideas. How would *he* solve the problem of reconciling both sides' interests? As Neuharth later acknowledged, he should have asked Wyman for his ideas before telling him what the new name should be. Not only would Neuharth have gotten Wyman involved, but he would have discovered how much importance CBS attached to keeping its name.

Once you have elicited your opponent's ideas, you need to build on them. This doesn't mean accepting them as they are. Rather, select the ideas you find most constructive, and starting with them, head off in the direction you want to go. It is easier to get your boss to change his position if you say "Building on your idea, what if we . . . ?" Or "I got this idea from something you said at the meeting the other day. . . ." Or "As a follow-up to our discussion this morning, it occurred to me that . . ." Show your counterpart how your proposal stems from or relates to one of *his* ideas.

Building on his ideas does not mean shortchanging your own. It means building a bridge from his thinking back to yours. Keep in mind the seventeenth century abbot about whom the Pope said, "When the conversation began, he was always of my opinion, and when it ended, I was always of his."

Ask for Constructive Criticism

As you develop your ideas, keep your opponent involved by inviting his criticism. Stress that you are asking not for a yes-or-no decision but for feedback. Encourage constructive comments by asking problem-solving questions, such as "Which interests of yours does this approach fail to satisfy?" "In what respect is it not fair?" "How would you improve on it?" and "Is there any way we can make it better for your side without making it worse for mine?"

Once you have elicited his suggestions, consider creating a joint draft that incorporates his ideas and your own. Then run it by him for further comments. In a multiparty negotiation, show it to all the relevant participants and invite their suggestions. Then revise the draft, and if necessary, ask for more criticism. Gradually you will build consensus. The process is a little like creating a mural together—your opponent paints a few strokes, you do, his boss does, yours does. Each person who gets involved begins to think of the draft as his own.

Offer Your Opponent a Choice

If your opponent resists telling you his ideas or giving you feedback on yours, try to involve him by offering him a choice. For instance, if he has been putting off talking with you, begin by asking him for small decisions: "Is ten o'clock on Tuesday better for you than three o'clock on Wednesday?" and "Would you prefer to meet at your office or mine?"

If he refuses to explore options for breaking the impasse, offer him a list of alternatives to choose from. If you are deadlocked over price, for example, tell him: "We can resolve the difference between your asking price and my offer by having an appraiser decide, *or* I can pay the difference with assets other than cash, *or* I can spread out the payments over time. Which approach would you prefer?" It may be easier for him to choose between A, B, and C than to invent D.

Once he selects an alternative, it becomes his idea. Take the example of the homeowner who was negotiating an agreement with a general contractor. Worried that the remodeling work on his house might take much longer than he planned, the homeowner proposed a twenty percent penalty for failure to finish on time. But the contractor refused. So the homeowner challenged him: "Okay, *you* name a date you're absolutely certain the job will be done." Put on the spot, the contractor picked a date three months after the scheduled completion. The homeowner then asked, "Okay, now will you agree to the clause?" Because the homeowner was only asking the contractor to live up to his own worst-case estimate, the contractor agreed.

The process of working together with your opponent can be long and arduous, but the rewards can be great. Remember the Chinese proverb: "Tell me, I may listen. Teach me, I may remember. Involve me, I will do it."

Satisfy Unmet Interests

Even if your opponent is fully involved in the process of shaping an agreement, he still may resist coming to terms. Often his resistance stems from an unmet interest that you have overlooked.

Take the acquisitions negotiator for Campbell's Soups who was trying to buy an extremely successful restaurant from its owner-manager. Campbell's was interested in starting a chain of such restaurants. The acquisitions negotiator started by making what he thought was a fair offer, but the owner rejected it. Over the ensuing six weeks the negotiator increased the offer several times but to no avail. The owner would not even make a counteroffer. The talks were at an impasse, and the negotiator was on the verge of giving up. He blamed the deadlock on the owner's difficult personality.

But then the negotiator decided to probe a little. In his next meeting with the owner, he backed off from his single-minded pursuit of a deal and encouraged the owner to discuss his reservations about selling the business. The owner said, "This business is my baby. And it has made me famous. I'm not sure I want to sell it and become part of your company. For one thing, I like running my own show. You're going to have to pay me a lot to make it worth my while to give it all up." The negotiator came to appreciate the owner's strong needs for autonomy and recognition, interests that were clearly not met by a deal in which the owner became a company employee.

So the negotiator asked the owner: "What if you don't become our employee? This would be a little unusual, but what if we form a joint venture together to own and operate the restaurant? Campbell's would purchase, say, eighty percent of the stock from you, and you would keep twenty percent. You would be president of the joint venture; you'd stay in charge. And we would agree to buy your twenty percent at some future time. The longer you stay, the more we would pay for your stock. Would something like this meet your needs?"

The owner's response was positive, and a deal was soon struck. His needs for recognition and autonomy were fulfilled, as was his interest in a decent price. Campbell's was able to acquire the restaurant at a reasonable cost and to retain the owner long enough to benefit from his successful management formula.

This story illustrates how useful it is to look for a creative solution. More important, it shows how easy it is to miss such a solution by overlooking your opponent's unmet interests. To address these interests, as the Campbell's negotiator did, you have to jettison three common assumptions: that your opponent is irrational and can't be satisfied, that all he basically wants is money, and that you can't meet his needs without undermining yours.

Don't Dismiss Your Opponent as Irrational

When you are frustrated by an inflexible opponent, it is easy to blame the impasse on his irrational nature: "My boss is crazy. No one can deal with him," or "Teenagers are just hopeless. It's no use reasoning with them." If you conclude that your opponent is impossible to deal with, you will not bother to probe for unmet interests.

It is easiest to reach this conclusion with hostage-takers: "You can't negotiate with terrorists—they're madmen." Certainly, their behavior may be irrational from our perspective, but it may make perfect sense from *theirs*. As long as there is a logical connection *in their eyes* between their interests and their actions, then we can influence them. One leading hostage negotiator, who represents corporations worldwide whenever their executives are seized, says, "They're all rational. Everyone negotiates. Even the 'dregs' give value for money." If hostage-takers are susceptible to being influenced, then your boss and teenager probably are too.

So don't give up easily. Put yourself in your opponent's shoes and ask yourself honestly: "Would I agree to this if I were he? Why not?" And remember that his values may differ from yours, which might lead him to reject what you consider acceptable. If you take a hard look, as the Campbell's negotiator did, you may well uncover interests that make it understandable from your opponent's perspective to say no.

Try to address your counterpart's objections and satisfy his interests while still meeting your own. Terrorists, for example, are usually motivated by the deep desire to get public recognition for their cause. Often the secret to persuading them to release hostages is to let them know that their message has been heard, and that killing the hostages would only discredit them in the eyes of the public. Many seemingly intractable hostage-taking incidents have ended after the terrorists received air time on TV and radio.

Don't Overlook Basic Human Needs

We often assume, as the Campbell's negotiator did at first, that our opponent is interested only in money or something equally tangible. We miss the *intangible* motivations that drive his behavior—his basic human needs. Everyone has a need for security and a deep desire for recognition. Everyone wants to identify with some group and have control over his own fate. Nations and ethnic groups have basic needs too. If unmet, these needs can block agreement.

By satisfying your opponent's basic human needs, you can often turn him around. The Campbell's negotiator was able to fulfill the restaurant owner's needs for recognition and autonomy. The young Steven Spielberg found a way to meet the bully's need to feel important. A hostage-taking in Boston ended after the authorities guaranteed that the hostage-taker would not be physically harmed. An impasse over a Wisconsin bank purchase was broken when the buyer agreed to keep the seller's name on the bank. An ethnic conflict in Italy's Trentino-Alto Adige region was defused when the German-speaking minority was granted cultural and administrative autonomy.

Don't Assume a Fixed Pie

Even if you have identified your opponent's unmet interests, you may believe you cannot satisfy them without frustrating your own. You may be falsely assuming a "fixed pie" —that more for your opponent means less for you. Frequently, however, you can expand the pie and satisfy your opponent's unmet interests at no cost and possibly some benefit to yourself.

Look for low-cost, high-benefit trades. The most common way to expand the pie is to make a low-cost, high-benefit trade. Identify items you could give your opponent that are of high benefit to him but low cost to you. In return, seek items that are of high benefit to you but low cost to him.

Consider a negotiation between an American businessman and a Moscow cabdriver. In broken Russian, the businessman inquired what the fare would be from the airport to the Rossia hotel. "Forty rubles," replied the cabbie. The price—equivalent at the time to sixty dollars—seemed high to the businessman, but when he asked another taxi driver, he was quoted the same fare. He then went back into the airport and bought a twenty-dollar bottle of vodka at a foreign currency store. He offered it to the first cabbie in lieu of payment, and the cabbie eagerly accepted. Why? Because the Russian would have had to wait in a four-hour line to buy the same bottle in a local liquor store. The vodka was low cost to the American, high benefit to the Russian. The cab ride was low cost to the Russian and high benefit to the American.

Use an if-then formula. Another way to expand the pie is to use an "if-then" formula. Suppose that you are a marketing consultant negotiating with a client over your fee. You would normally charge fifteen thousand dollars, but your client is unwilling to pay more than ten thousand. His resistance stems largely from his uncertainty about whether your efforts will truly help him. Instead of trying to persuade him that he is wrong, address his skepticism with an if-then formula: "What do you say we make my fee ten thousand dollars as a base, but *if* your sales increase twenty percent over the next six months, *then* you agree to add a ten-thousand-dollar bonus?" Your client readily agrees, because the increased sales would make it easy to justify paying you the bonus. You take a risk, but if you are successful, you stand to earn even more than you originally requested. In sum, don't fight your opponent's skepticism; take advantage of it by inventing a pie-expanding solution.

Help Your Opponent Save Face

Even if you are able to satisfy your opponent's substantive interests, he still may not agree. After all, a negotiation does not take place in a social vacuum. There is always a constituency or audience whose opinion your opponent cares about: his boss, his organization, his colleagues, his family and friends, or his own internal critic. Naturally he doesn't want them to think he has given in. If he has previously taken a public position and then does an about-face, his constituents might say, "You sold out!" "What kind of negotiator are you?" or "You let him rob us blind!" Your opponent's inflexibility may stem from constraints imposed by his constituents, rather than from his own concerns.

You may think, "Let him worry about *his* critics, and I'll worry about mine." But since his people can obstruct the agreement you want, it is your job to help him deal with them. Their criticism typically boils down to two arguments: that he has backed down from his original position and that the new proposal is unsatisfactory. Your challenge is to help him avoid both criticisms.

Help Him Back Away Without Backing Down

Face-saving is at the core of the negotiation process. There is a popular misconception that a face-saving gesture is just a cosmetic effort made at the end of a negotiation to boost the other person's ego. But face is much more than ego. It is shorthand for a person's self-worth, his dignity, his sense of honor, his wish to act consistently with his principles and past statements, and, of course, his desire to look good to others. All these may be threatened if your opponent has to change his position. Your success in persuading him to do so will depend on how well you help him save face.

Consider the face-saving skill shown by French statesman Georges Clemenceau in negotiating for a statuette in an Oriental bazaar. The shopkeeper offered it to Clemenceau for "only" seventy-five rupees "because it's you." The Frenchman responded with a counteroffer of forty-five rupees. The haggling continued, but Clemenceau stuck to his initial offer. Eventually, the shopkeeper threw up his hands and protested, "Impossible! I'd rather give it to you!" "Done!" replied Clemenceau, pocketing the statuette. "You are exceptionally kind, and I thank you, but such a gift could only come from a friend. I hope you will not be insulted if I offer you a gift in return." The perplexed shopkeeper said he would not. "Here," said Clemenceau, seeking to help him save face, "are forty-five rupees for you to use in charitable works." The shopkeeper accepted the money, and they parted on excellent terms.

Show how circumstances have changed. One face-saving approach is to explain that originally your opponent may have been right but that circumstances have changed. Suppose your most important customer insists on revisions in your company's standard sales contract but the lawyer at company headquarters has told you there will be no alterations. Instead of challenging the lawyer's decision directly, identify new conditions that enable the lawyer to explain why he changed his mind: "Your no-changes policy has always been the right one for a regulated marketplace. Now that the Feds have deregulated this sector, however, we're facing much tougher competition. Do we really want to risk losing one of our biggest customers?"

Ask for a third-party recommendation. A time-honored method of face-saving is to call in a third party—a mediator, an independent expert, a mutual boss or friend. A proposal that is unacceptable coming from you may be acceptable if it comes from a third party.

Take the avid fisherman who wanted to buy a cabin in the North Woods. The owner insisted on an unrealistically high figure—$45,000—and announced he would not bargain. The fisherman tried hard to change the owner's mind but to no avail. So the fisherman finally said, "Okay, I'll pay whatever an appraiser determines to be the fair price for the house." The owner responded, "All right, but *I* pick the appraiser." The fisherman countered, "Okay, you pick an appraiser, and I'll pick an appraiser, and together the two can select a third." The owner agreed. They each identified appraisers who in turn chose the president of the local appraisers' society. Under the watchful eyes of his peers, he came up with a figure of $38,000. Muttering that the appraiser didn't know what he was doing, the stubborn owner nevertheless agreed to sell the cabin at that price. Having kept his pledge not to bargain, he hadn't lost any face.

Point to a standard of fairness. In the absence of a third party, you can use the next-best thing: a fair standard. Suppose you are at loggerheads with an insurance claims agent over compensation for your stolen car. He refuses to pay more than five thousand dollars but you think seven thousand is fair. So you say, "Why don't we let the market-place decide? You check the classified ads for similar cars, and I'll do the same. Let's talk again tomorrow." With the new information on hand, you agree on a figure of $6,500. He doesn't feel he is backing down, since he is simply deferring to the market price. He also has a legitimate explanation if his supervisor should question why he agreed to pay you the additional $1,500.

Help Write Your Opponent's Victory Speech

Your opponent's constituents may attack the proposed agreement as unsatisfactory. So think about how he can present it to them in the most positive light, perhaps even as a victory. What could you offer that would help him do so?

President John F. Kennedy and his advisers asked themselves this question in October 1962 as they searched for a way to make it easier for Soviet Premier Nikita Khrushchev to withdraw Soviet missiles from Cuba. Kennedy decided to offer Khrushchev his personal pledge that the United States would not invade Cuba. Since Kennedy had no intention of invading anyway, the promise was easy to make. But it allowed Khrushchev to announce to his constituents in the Communist world that he had successfully safeguarded the Cuban revolution from American attack. He was able to justify his decision to withdraw the missiles on the grounds that they had served their purpose.

Anticipate what your opponent's critics are likely to say and arm him with persuasive counterarguments. If, for example, you are an investment banker negotiating with your boss for a raise and bonus, think what your boss's partners might say if he agreed to your proposal: "You're being too lavish with the firm's money." "You're going to make us look bad when our people find out how well yours did." Then think of answers your boss could give: "He deserves it. He brought in five million dollars' worth of business last year." "If we don't reward him for his hard work, we'll lose him to the competition." When you ask your boss for more money, prepare him by raising likely criticisms and presenting the counterarguments.

At little or no cost to yourself, you may be able to help your opponent reframe a retreat as an advance. Suppose, for example, you are dealing with a union leader who has pledged to bring back a ten percent wage increase. You might agree to give him a four percent increase this year and a three percent increase for the next two years. He can tell his membership that he succeeded in obtaining a ten percent increase—over three years. Or suppose you are buying a house from someone who is determined to get $200,000 because that's what he paid for it, even though it is now worth only $180,000. You might agree to pay $200,000 but stretch out the payments over time so that the deal is equivalent to a $180,000 immediate payment.

Don't forget the value of giving credit. Even if the solution is your idea, consider letting your opponent share the credit—or take all of it. In Washington, D.C., a city full of politicians eager to claim good ideas as their own, there is a saying that goes: "There's no limit to how much you can accomplish in this town if you are willing to allow someone else to take the credit." The same holds true in negotiations. Take the bride who wanted to register for china. Her fiancé resisted, saying, "We don't need all that crockery." The china became a sore subject. In a goodwill gesture he accompanied her to the store, where he saw a pattern he liked. She happily agreed to his selection and gave him credit for the choice. He proudly announced to their families and friends that *he* had selected the china.

Even if there is nothing you can give your opponent, you can often shape appearances so that he does not seem to lose. When British Prime Minister Benjamin Disraeli was pestered by a supporter who wanted a noble title, Disraeli told him: "You know I cannot give you a baronetcy, but you can tell your friends that I offered you one and you refused it. That's much better."

Go Slow to Go Fast

Even if you can satisfy your opponent's interests and help him save face, he still may not agree because the process of reaching agreement seems too difficult. Too much needs to be decided in too short a time.

Your job is to make the process easy. Go slow in order to go fast. Think of yourself as a guide helping a client afraid of heights climb a steep mountain. Break the journey into small stages, pace your client, stop to rest when necessary, and look back periodically at how far you have come.

Guide Your Opponent Step by Step

If reaching agreement on the whole package seems impossible at first, try breaking the agreement up into steps. A step-by-step approach has the merit of making the impossible gradually seem possible. Each partial agreement can open up opportunities that were not evident at the outset.

Consider how far a step-by-step approach took American diplomat Charles Thayer in negotiating with a German prison director at the outbreak of World War II. Thayer, whose mission was to deliver some belongings and supplies to a British vice-consul being held prisoner, recalled:

> He [the prison director] had the British vice-consul brought from his cell, and one by one I handed over the items: pajamas, shirts, socks, and a toilet kit. . . . I then produced a bottle of sherry, explaining that the vice-consul should have it served before his luncheon. The director said nothing, but took the bottle submissively. Next I produced a bottle of champagne which, I said, should be properly iced with the vice-consul's dinner. The director shifted uneasily but remained silent. Next came a bottle of gin, another of vermouth, and a cocktail shaker. This, I explained, was for the vice-consul's evening martini. "Now, you take one part of vermouth," I began, turning to the director, "and four parts of gin, add plenty of ice—" But I had reached the end of my tiny steps.
>
> *"Verdammt!"* the director exploded. "I am willing to serve sherry and champagne and even gin to this prisoner, but he can damn well mix his own martinis."

If Thayer had presented all his requests at once, the prison director would undoubtedly have rejected the whole lot. By taking a step-by-step approach, Thayer substantially accomplished his mission.

To break the ice at the start of a tense negotiation, begin, as Thayer did, with the issue that is easiest for you to agree on. By moving progressively from the easier to the more difficult issues, you can get your opponent in the habit of saying yes and show him that agreement is possible.

If your opponent is particularly skeptical, consider starting with an experiment. Suppose you have devised a solid proposal for a new project but your boss is reluctant to give you the go-ahead. To him, it seems simpler and safer to stick with the tried and true. To persuade him, make the agreement experimental: "Can we carry out a pilot project with one department?" or "Can we try it out for one month?" By reducing the risk, an experimental agreement makes it easier for your counterpart to say yes.

When you are in the thick of the negotiation, it is easy to lose perspective and grow disheartened. Identifying the expanding areas of agreement and the shrinking areas of disagreement can generate a sense of momentum. Pause at each step to sum up progress: "So we've essentially agreed on the product and price. All we have to decide is how we share the costs of service and delivery."

Don't Ask for a Final Commitment until the End

Sometimes the step-by-step approach won't work because your opponent is reluctant to make even a small agreement. "If I give an inch, he'll take a mile." If this is the case, don't press him for an immediate concession. Set him at ease by reassuring him that he need not make a final commitment until the very end when he can see exactly what he will get in return.

This is what President Jimmy Carter did during the 1978 Camp David negotiations on the Middle East. Both Israeli Prime Minister Menachem Begin and Egyptian President Anwar Sadat were reluctant to budge from their stated positions, fearing that any concession would be perceived as a sign of weakness. So Carter did not ask them to change their positions until the end of the thirteen days of peace talks. During that time he focused their attention on criticizing and continually improving an American discussion draft. After twenty-three drafts there seemed to be no way to make the draft better for one side without making it worse for the other. Only then did Carter ask Begin and Sadat for a decision. Instead of having to make many painful decisions along the way, each leader had to make only one at the end. Instead of facing a slippery slope, each could see exactly what he was going to get in return for his concessions. Begin saw that in exchange for relinquishing the Sinai, he would get peace with Egypt. Sadat saw that in return for making peace with Israel, he would get the Sinai back. Both leaders said yes.

If your opponent resists a step-by-step approach, make clear that *nothing* is agreed until *everything* is agreed.

Don't Rush to the Finish

The closing phase of a negotiation is often characterized by a rush. The business meeting is coming to an end. A strike deadline is pending. One of the parties needs to catch a plane. Or you may simply sense an agreement is near and begin to sprint toward it like a runner at the end of a race.

Whatever the reason for the rush, it is easy to make mistakes in this atmosphere. If you hurry your opponent, he will often react by exploding over something trivial or by suddenly finding fault with part of the agreement. In order not to lose him, you need to slow down, back off, and give him a chance to think.

Encourage him to consult with his constituents. They may have instructed him to maintain a rigid position. If he comes back with a very different agreement, they may well reject it. A caucus allows him to educate them about the merits of the proposed agreement and to secure their support.

In the rush, it is also easy to conclude that you have reached agreement when in fact you haven't. As your lawyers set to drafting the contract the following morning, they may discover that you and your opponent have different interpretations of the agreement. This can lead to accusations of bad faith that leave you worse off than if you hadn't declared agreement in the first place.

There is a simple way to avoid this problem. When you think you have reached agreement, take a moment to sum up: "Let's make sure we both have the same understanding of what we have agreed on." Then go over each issue carefully. If possible, set down your agreement in writing. Movie mogul Samuel Goldwyn once quipped, "A verbal contract isn't worth the paper it's written on." Whatever you do, make sure the terms are as clear and specific as possible. A little bit of clarity at this stage can prevent a lot of unnecessary misunderstanding later.

Across the Bridge

Building a golden bridge involves much more than making your opponent an attractive proposal. First, it means involving him in crafting the agreement. Second, it means looking beyond his obvious interests, such as money, to address his more intangible needs, such as recognition or autonomy. Third, it means helping him save face as he backs away from his initial position; it means finding a way for him to present the agreement to his constituents as a victory. And last, it means going slow to go fast, guiding him step by step across the bridge.

You have now made it as easy as possible for your opponent to say yes. If he crosses the bridge, congratulations. If he doesn't, however, you need to make it as *hard* as possible for him to say no. That is the subject of the next and final chapter.

STEP FIVE

Make It Hard to Say No

BRING THEM TO THEIR SENSES, NOT THEIR KNEES

The best general is the one who never fights.
—Sun Tzu

What if, despite all your efforts to build your opponent a golden bridge, he still refuses to come to agreement? Since the problem-solving game has not worked, your natural temptation is to abandon it and turn to the power game instead. You use all your power to force your opponent to do what you want him to do. A spouse threatens to file for divorce, a company sues its delinquent customer, a union goes on strike, or a nation goes to war.

In the power game, you switch from listening and acknowledging to threatening, from reframing your opponent's position to insisting on your own, and from building a golden bridge to forcing him down the gangplank. Instead of making it easier for him to say yes, you make it harder for him to say no. You escalate not only your means but also your ends. As you invest more of your resources in the battle, you naturally want more from your opponent to compensate for your efforts. Your goal shifts from mutual satisfaction to victory.

Step 5. *Make It Hard to Say No*

The power game is supposed to work as follows: You threaten or try to coerce your opponent and then he backs down. However, unless you have a decisive power advantage, he usually resists and fights back. He gets angry and hostile, reversing your attempts to disarm him. He clings even more stubbornly to his position, frustrating your efforts to change the game. He becomes increasingly resistant to reaching agreement, not only because you may be asking for more but because agreement would now mean accepting defeat.

The harder you make it for him to say no, the harder you make it for him to say yes. That is the power paradox.

You are thus forced at great cost to try to impose a solution on your opponent. As he strikes back, you typically escalate into a costly struggle. In pursuing the lawsuit, strike, or war, you spend a great deal of time and money, not to mention blood, sweat, and tears.

You can easily end up with a lose-lose outcome instead of the win-win result you sought. The spouse who threatens a divorce may end up with an empty home, the company that sues may lose a valued customer, the union that goes on strike may force the company into bankruptcy, and the nation that goes to war may bog down in a ruinous stalemate. "An eye for an eye and we all go blind," Mahatma Gandhi once said.

Even if you win the battle, you may lose the war. In the process you may destroy your relationship with your opponent. And he will often find a way to renege or retaliate the next time he is in a better power position. War—in its military, corporate, or domestic forms—is a high-priced method of handling disputes. That is why more than two thousand years ago, the great Chinese strategist Sun Tzu wrote: "To win one hundred victories in one hundred battles is not the acme of skill. To subdue the enemy without fighting is the acme of skill."

How can you use power to bring your adversary to terms without ending up in a costly fight? How can you use power constructively rather than destructively? How can you overcome the power paradox?

Use Power to Educate

The key mistake you make when you feel frustrated is to abandon the problem-solving game and turn to the power game instead.

Overcoming the power paradox means making it easier for your opponent to say yes *at the same time* that you make it harder for him to say no. Making it easy to say yes requires problem-solving negotiation; making it hard to say no requires exercising power. You don't need to choose between the two. You can do both.

Treat the exercise of power as an integral part of the problem-solving negotiation. Use power to bring your reluctant opponent to the table. Instead of seeking victory, aim for mutual satisfaction. *Instead of using power to bring your opponent to his knees, use power to bring him to his senses.*

If he refuses to come to terms despite all your efforts, it is usually because he believes he can win. He believes that his best alternative to negotiation—his BATNA—is superior to your golden bridge. You need to convince him that he is wrong.

Use your power to *educate* your opponent. Assume the mindset of a respectful counselor. Act as if your opponent has simply miscalculated how best to achieve his interests. Focus his attention on his interest in avoiding the negative consequences of no agreement. Don't try to impose your terms on him. Seek instead to shape his choice so that he makes a decision that is in his interest *and* yours.

Bringing him to his senses works in tandem with building him a golden bridge. The first underscores the costs of no agreement, while the second highlights the benefits of agreement. Your opponent faces a choice between accepting the consequences of no agreement and crossing the bridge. Your job is to keep sharpening that choice until he recognizes that the best way to satisfy his interests is to cross the bridge.

Let Your Opponent Know the Consequences

If your opponent does not understand the consequences of failing to reach agreement, you should begin by letting him know how serious they are.

Ask Reality-testing Questions

The best and cheapest way to educate your opponent is to let him teach himself. Ask him questions designed to get him to think through the impact of not reaching agreement. Let reality be his teacher.

When Chrysler Corporation was on the verge of bankruptcy in 1979, company president Lee Iacocca tried to negotiate with Congress for a loan guarantee. But most lawmakers strongly believed that government should not be in the business of bailing out private enterprises. In subsequent congressional hearings, Iacocca tried to bring skeptical legislators to their senses. To focus attention on the consequences of rejecting Chrysler's appeal, he asked "reality-testing" questions: "Would this country really be better off if Chrysler folded and the nation's unemployment rate went up another half of one percent overnight?

Would free enterprise really be served if Chrysler failed and tens of thousands of jobs were lost abroad?"

Citing the Treasury Department's estimate of how much the layoffs would cost the government in unemployment insurance and welfare payments in the first year alone, Iacocca told the lawmakers: "You guys have a choice. Do you want to pay the 2.7 billion dollars now, or do you want to guarantee half that amount with a good chance of getting it all back?"

In essence, Iacocca was asking "Do you want to accept the consequences of no agreement, or would you prefer to cross the golden bridge?" While the legislators opposed helping Chrysler on ideological grounds, they changed their minds when they recognized the real choice facing them. As Iacocca later wrote, when a member of Congress "realized how many people in his constituency depended upon Chrysler for their living, it was farewell ideology." Iacocca got the 1.5 billion dollar loan guarantee he needed.

The three most common reality-testing questions are:

"What do you think will happen if we don't agree?" The most obvious question is the one Iacocca asked Congress: "What will the costs be if we can't reach agreement?" If your opponent seems to be missing part of the picture, bring it up in the form of a question: "Have you considered the possibility that a prolonged strike will put this company into bankruptcy and we will all lose our jobs?" or "Are you aware how serious the consequences will be for both of us if we don't settle this issue?" If your opponent has not focused on this problem or has underestimated the consequences, he may begin to appreciate just how attractive your golden bridge really is.

"What do you think I will do?" If you think your counterpart might be underestimating the strength of your BATNA, ask him: "If we can't reach agreement, what do you expect me to do to satisfy my interests?" or "What would you advise me to do?" A boss faced with an employee who has been missing work might ask, "What do you expect me to do if you're absent again?" or "What would *you* do if your employee was absent and you couldn't get the project done?" If you want to put it less personally, refer to your constituency. A union leader can ask his management counterpart: "How do you think the employees will feel about losing their health benefits, and what do you think they'll do about it?"

If your opponent has threatened you, ask him how he thinks you will respond if he carries out the threat: "Sure, you could go on strike, but if you do that, what would you expect us to do? Do you think we'll just sit on our hands?" Use questions to show him that you are not as vulnerable to his threat as he may think and that your logical countermove would leave both sides worse off. "We have a six-month inventory, and we'll be able to keep the plant running with management personnel. It will hurt us for sure, but it will hurt the workers more. So where will that leave us?" Let him know that if you reported his threat to your constituency, it would only backfire: "If I convey that to my board members, they'll feel they're being blackmailed and you won't find them easier to deal with."

"What will you do?" If you think your opponent is overestimating his alternative, question him about it: "What are you likely to do in the absence of agreement? How much will that cost you? How will that satisfy your interests?" Obviously he will tend to exaggerate the strength of his BATNA, so probe a little to expose its negative points:

"You could take this matter to court, of course, but how long will that take? And what about the legal expenses? And even if you're sure you're right, will a jury necessarily see it your way?"

Warn, Don't Threaten

Asking questions may not always be enough to educate your opponent about the realities of failing to reach agreement. The next step is to use a direct statement of what will happen. Before proceeding with your BATNA, you should let your opponent know what you intend to do. You want to give him a chance to reconsider his refusal to negotiate. Indeed, a warning can be more effective than actually using your BATNA—since your alternative may loom larger in your adversary's imagination than it will in reality.

You need to be careful, however, not to threaten your opponent. A threat can easily backfire, changing the issue from a matter of dollars and cents to a test of his power and reputation. The raised stakes will make him fight back much harder. A direct threat will also tend to unify his organization against you. Internal differences will disappear as everyone joins forces to fight you, their common enemy.

How can you let your opponent know about your BATNA in a way that propels him to the negotiating table, not the battleground? The key lies in framing what you say as a *warning*, rather than a threat. At first sight, a warning appears to be similar to a threat, since both convey the negative consequences of no agreement. But there is a critical, if subtle, distinction: A threat appears subjective and confrontational, while a warning appears objective and respectful.

A threat is an announcement of your intention to inflict

pain, injury, or punishment on your opponent. It is a negative promise. A warning, in contrast, is an advance notice of danger. A threat comes across as what *you will do* to him if he does not agree. A warning comes across as *what will happen* if agreement is not reached. A warning, in other words, puts some distance between you and your BATNA. It objectifies the consequences of no agreement, so that they appear to result from the situation itself. It is easier for your opponent to bend to objective reality than to back down to you personally.

While a threat is confrontational in manner, a warning is delivered with respect. Present your information in a neutral tone and let your opponent make up his own mind. The more dire the warning, the more respect you need to show.

A threat is telling your counterpart in manufacturing: "If you don't agree to increase production, I'm going to take it up with headquarters." He is likely to react: "Who do you think you are, telling me how to run my department?" He may get angry, and you may be dragged into a corporate brawl. A warning, in contrast, is telling your counterpart: "If the agreed-upon production quota isn't met, this division will really suffer, and we'll all be in trouble with headquarters." You are more likely to induce him this way to return to problem-solving negotiation.

Sometimes you need to use a deadline to force a decision. Yet an arbitrary deadline may be interpreted as a threat. It is more effective to build in "natural" deadlines, which serve as objective warnings. Such deadlines might be this year's budget decision, the quarterly board of directors meeting, an upcoming press report, or the approach of Christmas holidays. These dates appear to be beyond your control, and thus are easier for your opponent to accept.

Demonstrate Your BATNA

If your opponent ignores your warning, you will need to take the next step: Make your power credible by demonstrating your BATNA. A demonstration shows what you plan to do without your having to carry it out. It educates your opponent at minimum cost to you and minimum pain to him.

In Japan, for instance, workers often carry on a "strike" while they continue working. They wear black armbands in order to let management know the depth of their grievances. The armbands also remind management how much potential power the employees wield over the economic future of the company. Such symbolic strikes have proven surprisingly effective in bringing management to the table for serious negotiations about workers' grievances.

If your BATNA is to go to court, you can demonstrate it by involving a lawyer in the negotiation. One neighborhood association, intent on persuading a resistant highway department to build underpasses rather than highly visible overpasses, hired a prominent lawyer to accompany its spokesperson as he delivered a petition to the department. Not a word was said about taking the dispute to court, but the message came through loud and clear. The highway department decided to reverse its original decision.

To demonstrate your BATNA in the midst of negotiations, you can walk out. This tactic is not to be used lightly. You should not be bluffing but rather sending your opponent and his constituents a strong signal that you are serious about resorting to your BATNA. When you walk out, you do not need to slam the door. Just say, "I'm sorry, but the way in which we have been negotiating is not likely to lead to a constructive outcome. I'm ready to negotiate anytime you are. Here's my phone number. Please give me a call when you're ready. Until then, I guess I'll have to pursue my alternatives." Leave the door open for your opponent to call you back, or for your boss to call his boss or for a third party to bring you back together.

Another way to demonstrate your BATNA is to prepare to carry it out so that your opponent discovers your plans in advance. Take the situation of an exclusive department store that had a discriminatory employment policy, hiring minorities only for the most menial jobs. A community organization protested, but the store refused to negotiate. In response, the organization mobilized three thousand minority shoppers and planned to bus them, dressed up in their finest clothes, to the store on one of its busiest Saturdays. The shoppers would browse for hours, keeping the salespeople occupied. The store's regular clientele would enter, take one look at the milling crowd, and leave. The leaders of the community organization included in their planning sessions someone who they knew would leak their plans to the store. When the store managers learned of the scheme, they requested immediate negotiations with the community organization and quickly agreed to hire a sizable number of minority salespeople and executive trainees.

Remember that power, like beauty, exists in the eyes of the beholder. If your BATNA is to have its intended educational effect of bringing your opponent back to the table, he needs to be impressed with its reality.

Use Your BATNA, Defuse the Reaction

If your opponent persists in his refusal to negotiate, you have no choice but to use your BATNA. The dissatisfied workers would strike. The neighborhood association would file a lawsuit against the highway department. The community organization would carry out its shopping expedition to the department store. The marketing chief would ask headquarters to order the manufacturing division to increase production.

The problem, however, is that your open exercise of power is likely to provoke your opponent into fighting back, even when his doing so makes no sense. His emotions may take over, blinding him to the costs of fighting and the benefits of negotiating. His "irrational" resistance may end up frustrating your attempt to educate him through the use of power.

How you use power is therefore all-important. *The more power you use, the more you need to defuse your opponent's resistance.*

Deploy Your BATNA Without Provoking

Power lends itself to abuse. The exercise of power can easily become an escape valve for your pent-up feelings of frustration and anger. You probably have a natural human desire to make your opponent pay for all the grief he has caused you. Yet for every action you take, there is likely to be an equal and opposite reaction on his part. "The more brutal your methods," wrote Sir Basil Liddell Hart, a noted British military strategist, "the more bitter you will make your opponents, with the natural result of hardening the resistance you are trying to overcome."

Use the minimum power necessary. Next to not using your BATNA at all, the best approach is to use it as little as possible. Use the minimum power necessary to persuade your opponent to return to the negotiating table. Usually this means exhausting all your alternatives before escalating. At the outset of the Cuban missile crisis, President

Kennedy decided against ordering an immediate airstrike on the Soviet missiles in Cuba. He wanted to avoid provoking Premier Khrushchev into ordering a counterstrike against U.S. forces in Berlin or Turkey that might, in turn, escalate into World War III. To display his power without ratcheting up the stakes, Kennedy resorted first to a naval blockade around Cuba. His strategy paid off. The crisis was resolved through negotiation, not war.

The more restraint you exercise, the less negative your opponent's reaction is likely to be. If you are a striking union, keep the strike peaceful; stop your hotheads from engaging in physical violence or industrial sabotage. If you are the employer, think hard before hiring replacements for the strikers. Go out of your way not to provoke your opponent, remembering that your ultimate goal is to bring him to the negotiating table.

When faced with a Communist rebellion in Malaysia in 1948, Winston Churchill summoned Field Marshal Templeton and gave him full authority to do whatever he needed to quash the rebellion. Churchill had one piece of advice, however, for the field marshal: "Absolute power, Templeton . . . heady stuff . . . Use it sparingly."

Use legitimate means. The more legitimate your use of power, the less likely your opponent will resist it, and the more likely it will induce him to negotiate. In the case of the discriminatory department store, for example, shopping was perfectly legal, and management could not keep out the minority shoppers without generating negative publicity about the store and its hiring policies. In the Cuban missile crisis, President Kennedy chose to use a naval blockade, in good part because he believed it would be a more legitimate means than an airstrike. Legitimacy depersonalizes the use of power; your opponent is less likely to feel personally challenged and compelled to react.

Neutralize Your Opponent's Attack

A power contest is a two-way street. Your opponent may strike at you in retaliation for your power move or simply in order to force you to accept his terms. You will need to defend yourself. Counterattacking, however, will often result in a futile confrontation. The more effective approach is to *neutralize* your opponent's attack without striking back.

If you think your customer will threaten to go over your head to get a better deal, talk to your boss beforehand. Secure his commitment that he will refer the customer back to you. When the customer makes his threat, you are ready: "Please feel free to talk to my boss. I have already discussed the matter with him, and I'm confident he will tell you the same thing I have." Without attacking the customer, *neutralize* his ability to coerce you.

Consider the case of a coal mine with troubled labor-management relations. The mine was beset by bomb threats telephoned in to the switchboard just as the shifts were changing. Management would have to respond by closing the mine while a search was conducted. Finally, mine officials hit on the idea of instructing the switchboard operator to record the calls and tell callers: "Your voice is being recorded. How can I help you?" The first recorded bomb threat was played to the assembled miners, who were asked to let management know if they recognized the voice. After that, the number of bomb threats dropped off drastically. Management had effectively neutralized the caller's tactic.

Or consider an international example. In 1948, Soviet leader Joseph Stalin blockaded West Berlin, demanding that Allied troops leave the city. The Western powers considered breaking the blockade with an armed convoy but feared triggering World War III. Instead, they chose to neutralize the blockade by mounting an enormous airlift of food and supplies to the beleaguered Berliners. Realizing the blockade was not working, Stalin finally called it off and agreed to negotiate.

As each of these situations illustrates, your challenge is to foil your opponent's attack without attacking back. Your goal is not to punish him but to show him he can satisfy his interests only through negotiation.

Tap the Third Force

You may not have enough leverage by yourself. Fortunately, almost every negotiation takes place within a larger community that constitutes a potential "third force" in your negotiation. Involving other people is often the most effective way to deter your opponent's attacks and bring him to agreement without provoking a counterreaction.

Build a coalition. Whether you are inducing a dictator, a department store, or a difficult boss to negotiate, it is helpful to build a powerful coalition of supporters. The United States stood together in the Berlin crisis with Great Britain and France. The neighborhood association obtained the services of a prominent lawyer. The minority community organization was able to mobilize three thousand shoppers. In identifying potential allies, consider those most likely to sympathize with and lend support to your cause: a trusted friend or relative, a longstanding client, an organization that shares your goals, or someone who has experienced similar problems with your opponent.

While we naturally think of turning to our friends and allies, we rarely consider appealing to the other side's constituency—his family, friends, co-workers, and clients. Your opponent may not listen to you, but his constituents might. And he may well listen to them if they urge him to negotiate. In domestic hostage negotiations, for example, the police often use family members and friends to talk the hostage-taker into acting sensibly; in international cases, nations with ties to the hostage-taking group are often asked to intercede.

In addition to your allies and theirs, you can mobilize the people in the middle, the undecideds, the neutrals. If you are negotiating with your departmental rival over who will take the lead on a new project, the person in the middle may be your mutual boss. If you are a community organization trying to negotiate with a recalcitrant developer, you may turn to the media for coverage and supportive editorials.

Use third parties to stop attacks. The presence of a third party can deter your opponent from threatening or attacking you. When children are quarreling, the watchful eye of a parent will often prevent fisticuffs. When the general public is watching, even a dictatorial government may hesitate before using violence on protesters.

Consider an extraordinary negotiation. In 1943 hundreds of German women married to Jewish men marched for more than a week in the streets of Berlin. They sought to free their husbands from Nazi prisons where the men were awaiting transport to the gas chambers. The Nazis trained machine guns on the women, but they would not budge. They presented the Nazis with a dilemma: Release the prisoners or use violence on "Aryan" women in full view of a citizenry whose support and morale the Nazis were anxious to preserve. In the end, the most barbaric of governments chose the first option and approximately fifteen hundred Jews were saved from death. The women were able to deploy their BATNA—the street march—while inhibiting a negative reaction—a machine-gun slaughter—

because of the presence of third parties—the German public.

Use third parties to promote negotiation. Third parties can also induce your opponent to negotiate with you. The CEO can tell you and your rival vice-president that he wants you to resolve your dispute within a week. A judge can call you and your opposing counsel into his chambers and press you to reach a settlement out of court. Sometimes just the knowledge that others are watching is enough to bring your opponent to the table.

A third party can also help you settle your dispute by mediating. He can help each of you to understand the other's interests and can suggest possible options for agreement. Your opponent will usually find it easier to accept a mediator's solution than to give in to you. And if you are not on speaking terms, a third party can bring you together. The mediator may be a mutual friend, your common boss, a community leader, or a professional neutral.

If your counterpart refuses to agree to your proposal, you can elicit the support of others in making him see its wisdom. Consider the intervention approach commonly used in persuading alcoholics to seek treatment. A long-suffering wife, for instance, was faced with an alcoholic husband who repeatedly broke his promises to stop drinking. In desperation she turned to others for help: his children, siblings, closest friends, and employer. Together they confronted the alcoholic to persuade him to seek treatment. One by one they told him how much he meant to them and recounted specific incidents of dangerous driving, personal violence, or embarrassing behavior. They then collectively insisted he seek help. To make his decision easier, they had already prepared a list of treatment centers and made reservations for him at each. Faced with this outpouring of concern and support, he at last decided to accept the help he needed. The wife's effort would not have been enough; it took the urging of his friends, relatives, and colleagues. As the old adage puts it: "If one person tells you that you have a tail, you laugh. If three people tell you, you turn around to look!"

Other parties are more likely to help if you can show them you have a legitimate case. Bring to bear independent standards, such as past precedent, equity, company rules, and the law. Just being right is usually not enough, so frame your dispute as one in which the issue or principle is important to the third party. If you turn to your boss, you are more likely to win his support if you can show him how his personal interests or the larger interests of the company are at stake.

If the other party is not inclined to help bring your opponent to agreement, you may need to give him a reason to care. Consider the tactic adopted by tenants living in a slum building. They were trying to persuade the landlord to repair the broken plumbing, but he refused to listen. So the tenants decided to picket. Rather than carry their signs around the building or the landlord's office, they went to his home in an exclusive suburb. Within minutes the landlord was deluged with calls from his neighbors, who said, "I don't care how you make your money. Just get those people off our sidewalk." Not surprisingly, he agreed to repair the plumbing.

When resorting to your BATNA, don't overlook the useful role third parties can play in bringing your opponent back to the table. If you exert your power through them, you are less likely to trigger a strong negative reaction from your opponent.

Keep Sharpening Your Opponent's Choice

As you educate your opponent about the costs of no agreement, you need to remind him continually of the golden bridge you have built for him. When he refuses to negotiate, you understandably feel tempted to draw up the bridge —to rescind your last best offer. In fact, you ought to leave your most generous offer on the table in full view. Nothing will do more to reduce his resistance than the possibility of an attractive way out.

Your power to bring him to terms comes not from the costs you are able to impose but from the *contrast* between the consequences of no agreement and the allure of the golden bridge. Your job is to keep sharpening the contrast until he realizes that the best way to satisfy his interests is to cross the bridge.

Let Your Opponent Know He Has a Way Out

Power is useless if it drives your opponent into a corner and makes him resist you with all his might. Leaving him a way out is a time-honored precept. In the military chronicles of ancient China, the story is recorded of a general who surrounded a group of rebels at a city called Yuan Wu. Unable to capture the city, the general was reprimanded by his king: "Now you have massed troops and encircled the enemy, who is determined to fight to the death. This is no strategy! You should lift the siege. Let them know that an escape route is open, and they will flee and disperse. Then any village constable will be able to capture them!" The general followed this advice and took Yuan Wu.

Although you may assume your opponent knows of the way out, he may have become convinced that the way out no longer exists. A bank robber who has taken hostages may believe that, because he has shot a police officer in a gunfight, he has nothing more to lose from killing his hostages. It is the job of the police negotiator to reassure him that he can still salvage something by negotiating. A teenager who has stolen money from his parents to buy drugs may not believe he will ever be welcomed back into the family; it is the parents' challenge to convince him that he can come home.

It is easy for your opponent to misread your attempt to educate him through power as an attempt to defeat him. You need to reassure him constantly that your aim is mutual satisfaction, not victory. In a negotiation over a raise, your boss could interpret your bringing up an attractive job offer as a threat to leave. You will need to go out of your way to reassure him that you want to stay. *For every ounce of power you use, you need to add an ounce of conciliation.*

Let Your Opponent Choose

Paradoxically, just when your opponent appears to be coming around, you are well advised to back off and let him make his own decision. Respect his freedom to choose between the consequences of no agreement and the golden bridge. In the final analysis, the choice must be his. When family members and friends confront an alcoholic in an organized intervention, they urge him to seek help, describe the consequences of his not agreeing, but ultimately respect his freedom to choose.

Don't just give your opponent an either/or decision. Allow him to shape the details. Although the family may have packed the alcoholic's bags and made reservations for his treatment, they leave him with a choice of at least two treatment centers. This lets him assume ownership of the decision.

Even When You Can Win, Negotiate

An imposed outcome is an unstable one. Even if you have a decisive power advantage, you should think twice before lunging for victory and imposing a humiliating settlement on your opponent. Not only will he resist all the more, but he may try to undermine or reverse the outcome at the first opportunity. Earlier this century, the world learned this lesson at enormous cost; an imposed peace after World War I broke down and led to World War II.

The most stable and satisfactory outcomes, even for the stronger party, are usually those achieved by negotiation. Benjamin Disraeli, the nineteenth-century British Prime Minister, summed up the lesson for negotiators: "Next to knowing when to seize an advantage, the next most important thing is knowing when to forgo an advantage." In the midst of a power contest, it is vital for you to remember that your purpose is not victory through superior power but satisfaction through superior negotiation.

Consider how a small city in Texas sought to negotiate with a major oil company over the taxes to be paid by an oil refinery just outside the city limits. The citizens felt dissatisfied because their schools were poor, the roads bad, and community services inadequate. The city councilors pleaded with the company for a larger contribution to the city coffers, but the company refused—even though its tax rate was much lower than the rate paid by individual citizens.

There seemed little the city councilors could do. The company appeared to have all the power in the negotiation. It was one of the world's largest corporations, it was the town's biggest employer, and it was represented by shrewd and tough lawyers.

In desperation, the citizens held a meeting to decide

what to do. After much discussion, a local lawyer came up with an unusual proposal: "State law allows the town to expand the city limits if three quarters of the residents approve. Why don't we just annex the land on which the oil refinery stands? Applying the city tax rate should bring in the extra revenue we need." The idea was adopted, and the town held a referendum that was overwhelmingly approved.

The city now had a powerful BATNA. The councilors decided, however, *not* to put it into effect. They didn't want to antagonize the company—they just wanted it to assume a fairer share of the city's tax burden. So when they sat down to negotiate with the company's lawyers, they said, "We recognize all you have done for the good of the town. We couldn't survive without you. But, as you know, people feel very unhappy about our schools and roads, and they don't see why your company shouldn't pay at the same rate as everyone else. The law allows us to annex the refinery land, in which case you would have to pay the city tax rate. But we'd rather reach an agreement that satisfies your interests better."

The councilors went on to discuss mutually beneficial ways to make the tax less burdensome. They offered a tax break on future investment in the refinery, recognizing that this would boost the city's economy. Knowing of the company's campaign to attract its suppliers to relocate near the refinery, they offered a five-year tax holiday for new industries. In short, they tried to build a golden bridge for the company.

What could the company do? The referendum made it impossible to ignore the town's needs. The company's BATNA—moving the refinery—was far too costly. The company could, of course, retaliate by scaling down operations and canceling its contributions to local charities. But the councilors weren't just trying to squeeze it for money; the city was facing a genuine financial crisis. The councilors defused the company's reaction by going out of their way not to impose a solution, and by seeking instead to satisfy the company's interests.

In the end, the city and the company came to terms. The company agreed to increase its tax contribution from $300,000 to $2,300,000 a year. Rather than continuing to deteriorate, relations between the city and the company began to improve.

Forge a Lasting Agreement

Assuming you are successful in bringing your opponent to terms, you are now faced with one final challenge: translating his newfound willingness to negotiate into a firm and lasting agreement.

Keep Implementation in Mind

Even if your opponent agrees, he may not carry out the terms. A delinquent customer may promise you that, "The check will be in the mail tomorrow." A bankrupt business-person may claim, "I'm sure receipts will come in next week." But can you rely on their words?

You need to design an agreement that induces your opponent to keep his word and protects you if he doesn't. You don't need to act distrustful; act *independently* of trust.

Design the deal to minimize your risks. Don't just rely on a court to enforce your agreement; litigation can be long and costly. If you have doubts about your opponent's reliability, structure the deal so you don't have to carry out your side of the agreement until he fulfills his. If you are a buyer, arrange to delay your payments or put them in escrow until the seller has delivered all he has promised and you have checked it over. If you have recently made a sale to an erratic customer, don't build up a lot of inventory for his sake. Wait until he develops a track record of prompt payment.

To protect yourself further, you can build guarantees into the agreement. Instead of relying on someone's promise to buy your house or company, ask for a nonrefundable security deposit. If you are being hired into an uncertain job, propose a "golden parachute" clause that specifies what you will receive if the company folds or you are fired.

Make it more difficult for your opponent to back out by involving others. Try to secure the signatures of the key players on the other side. Invite people or institutions that your counterpart cares about to witness the agreement. Announce the deal publicly.

Don't let him treat your doubts as a personal attack. If he says "Trust me," tell him "Of course I trust you," and explain that it is just normal business practice: "Personally I am sure nothing will go wrong with our arrangements, but my lawyer insists on the routine of including the following guarantees." Or, if your future employer insists a handshake and an oral promise of a golden parachute are sufficient, say, "You're absolutely right, and I have full faith in what you are saying. Writing a memo to the file will be helpful, however, if you're promoted tomorrow and I get a new boss."

Build in a dispute resolution procedure. Guarantees offer you a *final* resort if your opponent breaks the agreement—but they don't give you a *first* resort. For that, you need to establish in advance a dispute resolution procedure. Your contract should spell out exactly what will happen if one party feels the other is not living up to the terms of the agreement.

A typical dispute resolution procedure might specify that you will first try to negotiate a resolution of your differences. If, after thirty days, you are unable to reach agreement, you will call in a mediator. If he is unsuccessful in thirty more days, you will submit your dispute to binding arbitration by a mutually acceptable third party. Oil companies about to engage in a joint venture have set up partnership committees to handle any disagreements that arise; if a dispute persists, it is referred to two senior executives, one from each company, who try to mediate a settlement. Only if that fails do the companies resort to arbitration. You should consider including a dispute resolution procedure in every agreement you make.

Reaffirm the Relationship

A difficult negotiation can easily strain your relationship. If your opponent leaves the table with sour feelings, he may not do a good job of selling the deal to his constituents or implementing it. He may carry out the letter but not the spirit of the agreement.

It is in your interest for your opponent to feel as satisfied as possible at the conclusion of the negotiation. Although you may feel elated at your success, don't crow. In the wake of the Cuban missile crisis, President Kennedy issued strict instructions to his Cabinet officers not to claim victory. He did not want to make it harder for Premier Khrushchev to justify to his comrades his decision to withdraw the missiles.

Be generous at the very end. Resist the natural temptation to fight over the last crumb. As a professional hostage negotiator put it: "We save some flexibility for the end because we like them to win the last round. We're easier at the end than they expect because we want them to think they did well." Your counterpart's satisfaction can pay off handsomely in the agreement's implementation as well as in future negotiations.

After a difficult negotiation you may feel that you never want to see your opponent again. Yet as long as you are dependent on him to carry out the terms of the accord, it is wise to preserve a good working relationship. Gracious words and symbolic gestures can help. If appropriate, organize a signing ceremony and a celebration for both sides. Check in with your counterpart regularly to make sure he thinks you are keeping up your side of the bargain. And deal promptly with any grievances he raises. The best guarantee of a lasting agreement is a good working relationship.

Aim for Mutual Satisfaction, Not Victory

The eminent Prussian military strategist Carl von Clausewitz looked upon war as a continuation of politics by other means. Similarly, you should treat power as a continuation of problem-solving negotiation by other means. Everything flows from that. You aim for mutual satisfaction instead of victory. You use power to educate rather than fight. You let your opponent know about the consequences of no agreement—through reality-testing questions, warnings rather than threats, and, if necessary, demonstrations of your power. Just as the best general never fights, so the best negotiator never uses his BATNA.

If you do have to use your BATNA, you use the minimum power necessary to induce your opponent to return to the table. You deploy your BATNA without provoking, and neutralize his attacks without attacking back. You work to defuse his reaction so he does not turn your use of power into a costly and futile battle.

You remind your opponent continually that the golden bridge is open to him. You do not seek to impose a solution but rather to educate him about the choice that is best for him—and for you. In short, you use power to bring him to his senses, not his knees.

Conclusion

Turning Adversaries into Partners

There is a story of a man who left seventeen camels to his three sons. He left half the camels to his eldest son, a third to his middle son, and a ninth to his youngest. The three set to dividing up their inheritance but couldn't negotiate a solution—because seventeen could not be divided by two or three or nine. The sons finally consulted a wise old woman. After pondering the problem, the old woman said, "See what happens if you take *my* camel." So then the sons had eighteen camels. The eldest son took his half—that was nine. The middle son took his third—that was six. And the youngest son took his ninth—that was two. Nine and six and two made seventeen. They had one camel left over. They gave it back to the wise old woman.

Like the seventeen camels, your negotiations will often seem intractable. Like the wise old woman, you will need to step back from the negotiation, look at the problem from a fresh angle, and find an eighteenth camel.

Breakthrough negotiation is such an eighteenth camel. It can help you reach agreement in negotiations that at first seem impossible. The challenge is to get past the usual obstacles: your own natural reaction, your opponent's negative emotions, his hardball tactics, his unsatisfied interests, and his belief that he can win through the exercise of power.

Consider how all five steps of the breakthrough strategy were applied in one of the most difficult situations imaginable: a hostage negotiation with an armed criminal.

A Hostage Negotiation

On Thursday morning, October 14, 1982, scores of police converged on the nation's second-largest medical facility, Kings County Hospital in Brooklyn, New York. A convicted armed robber named Larry Van Dyke was holed up in a basement locker room with five hospital employees. Van Dyke, who had just had a cast removed from a broken arm, had seized a gun from a corrections officer, shot and wounded him, and tried to escape. Cornered by police, Van Dyke had taken hostages. Almost immediately he had let one person go, instructing him to tell police: "I want out of here or I'm going to start killing people."

A decade earlier the police would probably have handled such an incident by using force. "In the old, old days," a police captain recalled, "we'd surround the place, give the guy the bullhorn, fire the tear gas, put on some type of flak jacket, and engage the guy in a firefight."

But instead of fighting, the police decided to talk. Detective Lieutenant Robert J. Louden, a trained hostage negotiator, began a conversation with Van Dyke by shouting through the closed locker-room door: "How ya doin'? My name's Bob and I'm here to see what's going on. I'm here to help sort this out and help us get out of this mess. What's your name?"

Van Dyke replied, "My name's Larry Van Dyke and I've got a whole roomful of people. I've got nothing to lose. I'm not going back to jail. You've got thirty minutes to give me my freedom."

Louden did not reject the demand or the deadline, but reframed them instead as aspirations: "I'll see what I can do. I'll look into it for you and get back to you as soon as I can. As you know, these things take time. It's not a decision I can make. In the meantime, is there anything *I* can get for you?" Louden was trying to refocus Van Dyke's attention on what was achievable.

As Louden was talking, a backup negotiator stood behind him. The backup's job was to prompt Louden with questions, pass him messages, and make sure he kept his emotional balance. It was Louden's way of going to the balcony.

Van Dyke warned that if the police tried an assault, he would kill the hostages. Louden assured him that no one was going to hurt him. "You don't know how we operate," the detective said. "In ten years no one's ever been hurt. We don't storm doors. It's not like TV." Van Dyke's lawyer counseled his client: "Larry, no one is going to hurt you. In three hundred cases, the hostage negotiation unit has never hurt anyone."

Van Dyke threatened to break out of the room with his hostages. Louden told him: "Larry, you're better off staying in. You've got us locked out and we've got you locked in. We've got plenty of people out here. We don't want to use force, but we will if we need to. You're smart. You know how the game is played. Let's see if we can work this out."

Louden asked open-ended questions to find out what Van Dyke was thinking and what he wanted: "How did you get into this mess? How can we sort it out?" Van Dyke started complaining about corruption and abuse in the state prison system. Louden listened sympathetically, saying, "I understand how you feel," "I've heard similar things from others," and "Because you've raised it, we may be able to launch an investigation into the corruption." He was trying to build rapport with Van Dyke, acknowledging his points and agreeing where possible; in effect, Louden stepped to Van Dyke's side.

Van Dyke demanded to talk to Bella English, a reporter from the *Daily News* whose writing he admired. Louden agreed to help find her and persuaded Van Dyke to accept a field telephone to make communication easier.

Step by step, the detective made progress. Bella English was flown to the site in a police helicopter. "We want you to go on the phone," Louden told her, "but please don't use negative words like 'hostage' or 'jail.'"

English introduced herself to Van Dyke and asked him why he wanted to talk to her. "Because you're a fair reporter," he replied. He told her that he faced a prison sentence of twenty-five years to life on robbery charges. Coached by Louden, English tried to reassure Van Dyke that this was not necessarily so. Shortly thereafter, Van Dyke agreed to let one hostage go as soon as he received pillows, blankets, and coffee. At 4:15 P.M., the hostage emerged.

Four hours later Van Dyke agreed to let another hostage go if radio station WOR allowed English to broadcast his gripes about prison conditions. A few minutes after the broadcast, Van Dyke released the second hostage. "That was real good," Van Dyke told English. "You just saved a life." "No," English replied, "*you* just saved a life."

Van Dyke then agreed to free a third hostage if WABC-TV broadcast a live message during the eleven o'clock evening news. The station complied, at the Police Department's request. On the air, the freed hostage conveyed a message of love from Van Dyke to his wife and said no one would be hurt, "as long as the police didn't provoke anything."

Shortly after midnight, however, Van Dyke's mood changed. The police heard him threatening a hostage: "Old man, get on your knees. I got a gun to his head here. I don't want to hurt anybody but if they treat me ridiculous, I'll act ridiculous." Van Dyke tried to fix the blame on Louden. "This ain't going quick enough. I'm going to kill these people and it will be your fault."

But Louden deflected the blame: "Bullshit, Larry. We're here to help. We're all in this together. But if you do that, it's not us. It's you. Now let's see if we can work this out." Louden constantly sought to redirect attention back to the problem.

On Friday morning, tensions rose. Van Dyke had asked for the morning newspapers, but became angry when he saw reports that he had been accused of informing on fellow inmates. "They blew it!" he screamed in rage. "They said I snitched on inmates and guards. Guards, correct. Inmates, no." He said he had been forced by prison guards to entrap other guards in drug deals, and claimed he would be killed if he was returned to state custody.

Louden tried to calm Van Dyke, addressing his basic need for security: "I know you're not an informant. Whoever gave that statement was wrong. All the media can hear me saying that. Let me see if I can work it so you don't have to go back to a *state* pen."

Louden contacted federal and state correction officials to explore whether Van Dyke could be transferred to a federal penitentiary. The tension began to dissipate when Mike Borum, a deputy state correction commissioner, came to tell Van Dyke that he would try to arrange a transfer. Van Dyke told his cousin, a corrections officer who had been brought to the scene: "I'm thinking of surrendering. They offered me a good deal." Louden had built Van Dyke a golden bridge to retreat across.

Van Dyke agreed to release a fourth hostage if WABC-TV and WINS radio agreed to broadcast the release live, and also let Van Dyke tell his side of the story. On the air he complained about state prison conditions: "I have been beat up, I have been set up."

Four hours later Van Dyke became morose, insisting he didn't want to return to jail. He told Louden: "I've got nothing to lose. We're going to play Russian roulette." Louden tried to reassure him and talked soothingly to him through the night.

Early Saturday morning Van Dyke finally agreed to release the final hostage in return for press coverage and Borum's public promise of a transfer. At eight o'clock Louden was able to report to Van Dyke that Borum was making his statement on WABC-TV. Twenty-five minutes later the last hostage was released. At eight-thirty, Van Dyke came out to surrender. He was granted his request to talk with the press. "I'm not a madman," he said. "I'm a man that was trying to get freedom. . . . I got caught. I'm here." Then police took him away to the Metropolitan Correction Center, a federal detention center in lower Manhattan.

After forty-seven hours, one of the longest and most dramatic hostage incidents in New York City history was over. "Personally, I couldn't have held out much longer," said Louden, hoarse and weary.

The outcome was a victory for the police, who were able to win the release of hostages, prevent bloodshed, and take the criminal back into custody. Louden said that he and other members of his team had finally persuaded Van Dyke to give up by "trying to build trust and confidence, trying to establish that we could treat each other as human beings and help each other out of this okay."

Van Dyke didn't win his freedom, but he won a public promise to be transferred to a federal prison. After he surrendered, Van Dyke gave police the highest compliment they could have hoped for: "They shot straight with me," he said.

Just as the best general never has to fight, so the police never had to use force. They used their power not to attack Van Dyke, but to contain him and educate him that his best alternative lay in surrendering peacefully. They brought him to his senses, not his knees.

The Five Steps of Breakthrough Negotiation

Whether you are negotiating with a hostage-taker, your boss, or your teenager, the basic principles remain the same. In summary, the five steps of breakthrough negotiation are:

1. Go to the Balcony. The first step is to control your own behavior. When your opponent says no or launches an attack, you may be stunned into giving in or counterattacking. So, suspend your reaction by naming the game. Then buy yourself time to think. Use the time to figure out your interests and your BATNA. Throughout the negotiation, keep your eyes on the prize. Instead of getting mad or getting even, focus on getting what you want. In short, go to the balcony.

2. Step to Their Side. Before you can negotiate, you must create a favorable climate. You need to defuse your opponent's anger, fear, and suspicions. He expects you to attack or to resist. So do the opposite: Listen to him, acknowledge his point, and agree with him wherever you can. Acknowledge his authority and competence, too. Disarm him by stepping to his side.

3. Don't Reject . . . Reframe. The next step is to change the game. Instead of rejecting your opponent's position—which usually only reinforces it—direct his attention to the problem of meeting each side's interests. Take whatever he says and reframe it as an attempt to deal with the problem. Ask problem-solving questions, such as "Why is it that you want that?" or "What would you do if you were in my shoes?" or "What if we were to . . . ?" Rather than trying to teach him yourself, let the problem be his teacher. Reframe his tactics, too: Go around stone walls, deflect attacks, and expose tricks. To change the game, change the frame.

4. Build Them a Golden Bridge. At last you're ready to negotiate. Your opponent, however, may stall, not yet convinced of the benefits of agreement. You may be tempted to push and insist, but this will probably lead him to harden and resist. Instead, do the opposite—draw him in the direction you would like him to go. Think of yourself as a mediator. Involve him in the process, incorporating his ideas. Try to identify and satisfy his unmet interests, particularly his basic human needs. Help him save face and make the outcome appear as a victory for him. Go slow to go fast. In sum, make it easy for him to say yes by building him a golden bridge.

5. Bring Them to Their Senses, Not Their Knees. If your opponent still resists and thinks he can win without negotiating, you must educate him to the contrary. You must make it hard for him to say no. You could use threats and force, but these often backfire; if you push him into a corner, he will likely lash out, throwing even more resources into the fight against you. Instead, educate him about the costs of not agreeing. Ask reality-testing questions, warn rather than threaten, and demonstrate your BATNA. Use it only if necessary and minimize his resistance by exercising restraint and reassuring him that your goal is mutual satisfaction, not victory. Make sure he knows the golden bridge is always open. In short, use power to bring him to his senses, not his knees.

The breakthrough strategy requires you to resist normal human temptations and do the opposite of what you usually feel like doing. It requires you to suspend your reaction when you feel like striking back, to listen when you feel like talking back, to ask questions when you feel like telling your opponent the answers, to bridge your differences when you feel like pushing for your way, and to educate when you feel like escalating.

At every turn the strategy calls on you to choose the path of indirection. You break through by going around your opponent's resistance, approaching him from the side, acting contrary to his expectations. The theme throughout the strategy is to treat your opponent with respect—not as an object to be pushed, but as a person to be persuaded. Rather than trying to change his mind by direct pressure, you change the environment in which he makes decisions. You let him draw his own conclusions and make his own choice. *Your goal is not to win over him but to win him over.*

From Adversaries to Partners

It takes two to tangle, but it takes only one to begin the process of untangling a knotty situation. It is within your power to transform your most difficult negotiations. During the American Civil War, Abraham Lincoln made a speech in which he referred sympathetically to the Southern rebels. An elderly lady, a staunch Unionist, upbraided him for speaking kindly of his enemies when he ought to be thinking of destroying them. His reply was classic: "Why, madam," Lincoln answered, "do I not destroy my enemies when I make them my friends?"

The breakthrough strategy is designed to do precisely that—to destroy your adversary by making him your partner in problem-solving negotiation.

Analytical Table of Contents

End Notes

Step One

17   The "balcony" is a metaphor: I owe the phrase "go to the balcony" to my friend Professor Ronald Heifetz, who uses it in his courses on leadership at Harvard's John F. Kennedy School of Government.

20   Your BATNA is your best alternative: The term BATNA comes from Roger Fisher and William Ury, *Getting to Yes* (Boston: Houghton-Mifflin, 1981).

25   You need to look for multiple clues: For a good discussion of recognizing lies, see Paul Ekman, *Telling Lies* (New York: Norton, 1985), and Suzette Haden Elgin, *Success with the Gentle Art of Verbal Self-Defense* (Englewood Cliffs, New Jersey: Prentice-Hall, 1989), pp. 28–29.

25   Cross-cultural misunderstanding: Sergei Khrushchev, personal communication to the author, February 1989.

27   "I was carrying him home": Quoted in "When Bad Bosses Happen to Good People," Jane Ciabattari, *Working Woman*, July 1989, pp. 88–89.

28   A movie producer: This example is adapted from a story told by screenwriter and humorist Larry Gelbart, cited in Carol Tavris's insightful book *Anger: The Misunderstood Emotion* (New York: Simon & Schuster, 1982), pp. 149–150.

End Notes

Step Two

35   "Rarely is it advisable": Fortune de Felice, "Negotiations or the Art of Negotiating," in I. William Zartman, ed., *The 50% Solution* (New Haven: Yale University Press, 1976), p. 56.

35   An AT&T sales team: This account comes from a personal conversation with an AT&T executive, autumn 1985.

37   "Everything has been said before": André Gide, *Le Traité du Narcisse,* 1891.

38   Consider a contract negotiation: This example comes from William F. Whyte's excellent case study *Pattern for Industrial Peace* (New York: Harper, 1951), pp. 87–88 and 182–183.

41   Former U.S. Defense Secretary Robert McNamara: Personal notes, Harvard-Soviet Conference on the Cuban Missile Crisis, January 1989.

42   "Take the Columbia law professor": From K. Hegland, "Why Teach Trial Advocacy?: An Essay on Never Ask Why," in "Humanistic Education in Law," monograph III, J. Himmelstein and H. Lesnick, eds. (New York: Columbia University School of Law, 1982), p. 69.

44   Consider how an American diplomat: This story is cited in Dr. Julius Segal, *Winning Life's Toughest Battles: Roots of Human Resilience* (New York: Ivy Books, 1986), p. 41.

45   Consider the example of a fund-raiser for the United Way: For this story I am indebted to Pedro Ferreira.

47   People also use different "sensory languages" : For further information about the importance of matching the other person's sensory orientation, see the work of John Grinder and Richard Bandler, e.g., *Frogs into Princes* (Moab, Utah: Real People Press, 1979).

51   Make I-statements, not you-statements: For an excellent discussion of this point as it applies to parents and children, see Dr. Thomas Gordon, *P.E.T.: Parent Effectiveness Training* (New York: Plume, 1975), pp. 115–138.

53   A leading child psychologist: Haim G. Ginott, *Between Parent and Child* (New York: Avon, 1956), p. 138.

Step Three

61   In 1979, the SALT II arms control treaty: This example comes from a conversation with Senator Joseph R. Biden, Jr., in May 1983.

69   In the acquisitions negotiation: Victor Kiam, *Going for It! How to Succeed as an Entrepreneur* (New York: William Morrow, 1986), p. 178.

73   "We like deadlines": E. C. "Mike" Ackerman, personal communication to the author, autumn 1987.

75   Take the eighteenth-century general: *The Little, Brown Book of Anecdotes*, Clifton Fadiman, general ed. (Boston: Little, Brown, 1985), p. 222.

83   If you are a CEO: For a good discussion of merger and acquisition negotiations, see James C. Freund, *The Acquisition Mating Dance* (Clifton, New Jersey: Prentice-Hall, 1987).

Step Four

87   A classic example is the failure: This account is drawn from Al Neuharth's memoir *Confessions of an S.O.B.* (New York: Doubleday, 1989).

90   "When I was about thirteen": Steven Spielberg, quoted in *Time*, July 15, 1985. I am grateful to Arthur Kanegis for bringing this example to my attention.

91   "I turn towards the other man": François Walder, *The Negotiators* (New York: McDowell, Obolensky, 1959), p. 12.

93   "When the conversation began": Fortune de Felice, *op. cit.*, p. 57.

95   Take the example of the homeowner: This story comes from Edward Lustig.

95   Take the acquisitions negotiator for Campbell's Soups: This account comes from a personal conversation with a Campbell's executive, autumn 1983.

97   "They're all rational": Ackerman, *op. cit.*

98   Often the secret: For a good discussion of hostage negotiation techniques, see G. Dwayne Fuselier, "A practical over-

view of hostage negotiation," *FBI Law Enforcement Bulletin,* vol. 50, July 1981.

101   Consider the face-saving skill: *The Little, Brown Book of Anec-dotes, op. cit.,* p. 129.

102   Take the avid fisherman: For this story, I am grateful to Joseph Haubenhofer.

105   When British Prime Minister Benjamin Disraeli: *The Little, Brown Book of Anecdotes, op. cit.,* p. 171.

105   Go Slow to Go Fast: I owe this phrase to Michael Doyle and David Straus. They use it in their path-breaking book *Making Meetings Work* (New York: Playboy Press, 1976).

106   He [the prison director]: Charles W. Thayer, *Diplomat* (New York: Harper, 1959), pp. 90–91.

Step Five

112   "To win one hundred victories": Sun Tzu, *The Art of War,* translated by Samuel B. Griffith (Oxford, England: Oxford University Press, 1963), p. 96.

114   When Chrysler Corporation was on the verge: Lee Iacocca, with William Novak, *Iacocca: An Autobiography* (New York: Bantam, 1984), pp. 218–219.

120   Take the situation of an exclusive department store: This example comes from Saul D. Alinsky, *Rules for Radicals* (New York: Vintage, 1972), pp. 146–147.

121   "The more brutal your methods": Basil Liddell Hart, *Strategy* (New York: Signet, 1974), p. 357.

121   At the outset of the Cuban missile crisis: For an excellent account of presidential decision-making in this crisis, see Graham T. Allison, *Essence of Decision* (Boston: Little, Brown, 1971), and Robert F. Kennedy, *Thirteen Days: A Memoir of the Cuban Missile Crisis* (New York: W. W. Norton, 1969).

122   "Absolute power, Templeton": For this Churchill anecdote, I am grateful to Ambassador Jamsheed Marker.

125   In 1943 hundreds of German women: This incident is described in a doctoral study by Nathan Stoltzfus of Harvard University. For a brief description of the protest, see

Nathan Stoltzfus, "The Women's Rosenstrasse Protest in Nazi Berlin," in *Nonviolent Sanctions* (Winter 1989/90), p. 3.

126   Consider the intervention approach: For a full discussion of the intervention technique, see Vernon E. Johnson, *Intervention* (Minneapolis: Johnson Institute Books, 1986).

127   Consider the tactic adopted by tenants: Alinsky, *op. cit.*, p. 144.

128   In the military chronicles of ancient China: Sun Tzu, *op. cit.*, p. 79.

134   A typical dispute resolution procedure: For a discussion of dispute resolution procedures, see William L. Ury, Jeanne M. Brett, and Stephen B. Goldberg, *Getting Disputes Resolved* (San Francisco: Jossey-Bass, 1988).

134   In the wake of the Cuban missile crisis: See Robert F. Kennedy, *op. cit.*, pp. 105–106.

135   "We save some flexibility for the end": Ackerman, *op. cit.*

Conclusion

138   A hostage negotiation: This case is drawn from newspaper accounts, and from a personal interview with retired Detective Lieutenant Robert J. Louden on February 8, 1991.

146   During the American Civil War: From the *Little, Brown Book of Anecdotes, op. cit.*, p. 360.

About the Author

William Ury co-founded and serves as associate director of Harvard's Program on Negotiation. He is co-author (with Roger Fisher) of *Getting to Yes: Negotiating Agreement Without Giving In*, a two-million-copy bestseller translated into twenty-two languages. He is also co-author (with Jeanne M. Brett and Stephen B. Goldberg) of *Getting Disputes Resolved: Designing Systems to Cut the Costs of Conflict*, which won the Center for Public Resources Book Award for excellence and innovation in alternative dispute resolution.

A specialist in negotiation and conflict resolution who has taught at Harvard Business School, Ury trains corporate executives, labor leaders, diplomats, and military officers. His clients range from AT&T and American Express to the State Department and the Pentagon. He has served as a mediator in business, labor, and international disputes.

As director of the Nuclear Negotiation Project at Harvard Law School, Ury authored *Beyond the Hotline: How Crisis Control Can Prevent Nuclear War*. He was a consultant to the White House on the creation of nuclear risk reduction centers in Washington and Moscow. Ury also served for five years as associate director of the Avoiding Nuclear War Project at Harvard's John F. Kennedy School of Government.

Ury received his B.A. from Yale College, and his M.A. and Ph.D. degrees from Harvard University.

Getting to Yes

WILLIAM URY & ROGER FISHER

With over 2 million copies sold in over 20 different languages, *Getting to Yes* is the most successful book on negotiation on the market!

Negotiation is a way of life for the majority of us. Whether we're at work, at home or simply going out, we want to participate in the decisions that affect us. Nowadays, hardly anyone gets through the day without a single negotiation, yet, few of us are armed with the effective, powerful negotiating skills that prevent stubborn haggling and ensure mutual problem-solving.

- Don't bargain over positions
- Separate people from the problem
- Insist on objective criteria
- What if they won't play?

These are just a few of the easily remembered principles Fisher and Ury present that will guide you to success, no matter what the other side does or whatever dirty tricks they resort to.

RANDOM HOUSE

BUSINESS BOOKS

FIND EVERYTHING UNDER ONE ROOF

Visit the Random House website and get connected with information on all your favourite books and authors

EXTRACTS from our latest bestsellers and selected backlist titles

COMPETITIONS AND PRIZE DRAWS – Win signed books, audiobooks, merchandise and more

AUTHOR EVENTS find out which of our authors are on tour and where you can catch them

LATEST NEWS on bestsellers, awards and new publications

MINISITES with exclusive special features dedicated to some of our authors and their titles

READING GROUPS Reading guides, great special features and all the info for your reading group needs on our dedicated site

LISTEN to extracts from the latest audiobook publications

WATCH video clips of interviews and readings with our authors

RANDOM HOUSE FAQS including advice for writers, job vacancies and all your common queries answered

Come home to Random House

www.randomhouse.co.uk